THE ABUSE OF LEARNING

THE MACMILLAN COMPANY
NEW YORK · BOSTON · CHICAGO · DALLAS
ATLANTA · SAN FRANCISCO

MACMILLAN AND CO., Limited
LONDON · BOMBAY · CALCUTTA · MADRAS
MELBOURNE

THE MACMILLAN COMPANY
OF CANADA, Limited
TORONTO

THE
ABUSE OF LEARNING

The Failure of the German University

BY

FREDERIC LILGE

THE MACMILLAN COMPANY · NEW YORK

1948

PREFACE

THIS BOOK was born from a very personal desire, though one which I am sure I share with many who are anxious for the education of modern man: to know the reasons for the catastrophe of German intellectual culture. That culture centered in the German universities which in their greatest period, the nineteenth century, were admired by nearly all the world. By studying the ideas and ideals that inspired, directed and finally corrupted the teaching of these institutions, I hope to shed some light on the way which, in little more than a century, has led from the noble dignity of the brothers Humboldt to the degraded life which today creeps in the ruined German cities.

Deeply though I learned to hate during the last fourteen years, as did others who had a living relation to what was good and great in German culture, I have not written to condemn but to understand. The ominous darkness which was still low on the horizon when I left Germany as a young student and which rose to fill the sky, has long oppressed my mind. Neither changes in geographical location nor human atmosphere had the power to dispel it. But they provided the necessary distance and detachment from which to undertake the task I had set myself.

Were the breakdown of German culture and education an isolated event, as some writers have been inclined to believe, the temptation to pronounce judgment rapidly would indeed be irresistible. But as a student of the general history of education I soon realized that the causes of what happened in Germany are also active elsewhere. Actuality there is potentiality here. Most of the problems on which German higher education foundered remain unsolved throughout the Western world and, in fact, throughout those parts of the entire world which, by contracting for the ideas and achievements of the West, have

v

also inherited its crises. For many decades now German science
and scholarship have been deeply admired and uncritically imitated in this country. But more and more the values of that
legacy, too often misused by its eager heirs, are being questioned,
and such questioning forms part of the self-criticism of American education which, I believe, is only in its beginning.

I have left it to the discretion of the reader to draw certain
parallels between the developments I have described and those
which are more familiar to him from modern American education. In many instances such parallels are obvious enough; their
meaning need not be hammered home. Besides, too many learned
digressions and cross-references would have weakened the force
of the drama of ideas which I was anxious to capture and to
pursue to its tragic ending.

CONTENTS

CHAPTER I

THE BRIEF FLOWERING OF
GERMAN HUMANISM

DURING the eighteenth century intellectual life in the German universities was generally at such a low ebb that scarcely anyone would then have been bold enough to predict a brilliant future for these institutions. Not all the German universities, it is true, were enfeebled by a sterile Scholasticism. Those of more recent origin, as, for example, Halle (1694) and Göttingen (1737), were even then making a beginning in modern scholarship and critical thought. Besides, there was Kant in far-away Königsberg. But these were exceptions. Most of the institutions carried on a drowsy, vegetating existence. Generally speaking, professors taught only what was in the books. Their thinking had hardened into convention and orthodoxy, and their teaching was a mechanical pedantic routine. Students seldom had access to books: university libraries were generally small, antiquated, in disorderly condition and often closed for the larger part of the week. Göttingen, which quickly rose to eminence under the leadership of Gerlach von Münchhausen, was the shining exception. There a new generation of scholars trained themselves with the help of a growing and well organized library which was admired throughout the German states. Göttingen and, to a lesser extent, Halle were the first German universities which acted upon the principle, to be generally recognized only later, that good teaching and independent inquiry supplement and perhaps even require each other. But with the majority the idea prevailed until near the end of the century that truth was something already known and that academic teaching consisted merely in handing it on to the coming generation.

It was this general academic sterility which became the chief object of the criticism of German humanists and idealists at the turn of the century. Long before, however, the universities had been reproached for their practical uselessness by the absolutist governments, whose very policies shared the blame for the want of intellectual productivity in the universities. Absolutist governments, benevolent and otherwise, regarded these institutions jealously as territorial possessions and expected them to work for the enhancement of national and dynastic prestige. The idea that universities should contribute to interstate, let alone international, exchange of thought and to the universal advance of knowledge contradicted the politics and economics of the time. The enlightened despots of Prussia especially, together with their devoted and efficiency-minded bureaucracy, thought of all institutions within their power, whether these were for manufacture or education, in terms of a narrow state utilitarianism. They saw their tasks in the internal improvement of the country, in centralizing its administration and in increasing its military power. In none of these tasks did the "medieval" universities—it was then that medieval became an opprobrious term—prove of any use. They should train, so these governments thought, an efficient and well-informed officialdom and make contributions to the practical development of the military and industrial enterprises in which the absolute state engaged. But these expectations continued to be disappointed, and it is therefore not surprising that the very existence of the universities should at times have hung by a mere thread. As late as 1806 when much thought had already been given to their reform, the Prussian Minister von Massow called them "anomalous institutions" which the state would do well to replace by separate professional schools.

These claims of the Prussian rulers had been supported by no less a man than Leibniz. He, too, had been convinced as early as the end of the seventeenth century that the universities were antiquated beyond reform and had suggested instead to the Elector of Brandenburg the establishment of an academy of science. Leibniz drew up a plan, and in 1700 the Societät der

Wissenschaften was founded in Berlin with Leibniz as its first president. Leibniz proclaimed that the primary aim of the Academy was the pursuit of scientific inquiry of such a nature as to improve state manufacture, commerce, administration, civil and military engineering.[1] Throughout all its activities, including those of a literary nature, the Academy was to follow a thoroughly practical interest. Unfortunately Leibniz's hopes were not fulfilled, and after his death in 1716 the Academy, although it remained in existence, became as obscure and unproductive an institution as the majority of the universities.

Disappointed and angered by its performance, King Frederick William I (1713–1740) treated its members with great contempt. Among other things, he appointed three of his court fools presidents of the Academy, and ordered its members about as if they were schoolboys, threatening to dismiss them unless they met and sent in their reports regularly. The professors at the universities fared no better. On one of his visits to Frankfort-on-the-Oder, the seat of one of the more decrepit Prussian universities, his Royal Highness, who liked crude practical jokes, ordered all professors to attend a public mock disputation staged by his fool Morgenstern. The only member of the faculty who refused to attend, a man of courage and a scholar of some merit, was grossly insulted by the King.[2] One might have expected this ruler to show greater respect at least for Halle, the leading German university during his reign. There Thomasius had given the first university lectures in German after 1694, had fought superstition and witchcraft as well as academic pedantry and mummery; and Christian Wolf was at the time teaching an "enlightened" philosophy with the principle that nothing existed without sufficient reason. But the King, informed by the enemies of Wolf that he was teaching "fatalist" doctrines, had the philosopher run out of town "on forty-eight hours' notice and under pain of the halter." That was in 1723. Respect for the freedom and dignity of the mind was obviously still a long way off in Prussia.

There was one institution of higher education which received the King's care and financial support, the Collegium Medico-Chirurgicum which he founded in 1724. Its purpose was to supply the Prussian army, which he was building, with surgeons. From primitive beginnings this college grew throughout the eighteenth century until it became the leading school of medicine and science in all the German states. It was finally incorporated in the new University of Berlin in 1810. The College offered its staff and students the use of numerous auxiliary institutions which the medical "faculties" of the universities usually lacked, such as a veterinary school, a hospital (the Charité), scientific collections, a botanical garden, the Royal library, and an anatomical theater which was always well supplied with human cadavers. In 1806 the College had an excellent teaching staff of seventeen full professors, and by that time many students came to finish their medical training in Berlin even if they had already obtained a degree in medicine in some university. In short, the superiority of the College over any university faculty of medicine, both in professional and scientific respects, was established. This played a part in the choice of Berlin as the seat of the new university in 1810.[3]

In addition to their being inefficient and a useless expense to the absolutist state, the universities were found wanting in another respect: they were regarded as places of uncivilized, uncouth life. This criticism was expressed by a number of intellectuals in Berlin toward the end of the century when the city became the center of the German Enlightenment. Berlin, previously a small, dull garrison town, rapidly expanded after the end of the Seven Years' War (1763). Its population and wealth increased, and with it came the beginning of an intellectual life in the Prussian capital. A number of free-lance writers appeared for the first time, newspapers, periodicals, and literary clubs were founded, and numerous public lectures on scientific, philosophical, and literary subjects revealed a broadening popular interest in knowledge. The salons of intelligent young women from the wealthy middle-class families, the most brilliant of them Jewish, became the meeting places of a new intelligentsia.⁴ In contrast with the budding cosmopolitanism and the urbanity of these circles, academic life in the provinces appeared offensively boorish and Philistine. In Göttingen alone, where young aristocrats and even young princes went to study, a more worldly society of better-mannered students and teachers established itself. It is no surprise, therefore, that ideas and plans were discussed in Berlin circles for replacing the provincial universities with a cosmopolitan center of learning and enlightenment. The best illustration of this trend of thought is a plan for the reform of higher education submitted to the Prussian Minister Beyme in 1800.⁵ The author, J. J. Engel, sometime royal tutor, director of a Berlin Gymnasium, and an active publicist of that era, urged the minister to break entirely with the academic traditions and to abolish examinations, degrees, university self-government, and student fraternities. He condemned the universities as medieval and clannish institutions exercising a monopoly over higher learning and thereby obstructing both the progress and the dissemination of knowledge. He added that educated families hesitated to send their sons to the provincial universities because of the coarsening influence to which they would there be subjected. He suggested, for these reasons, the establishment in Berlin of an "unacademic" institution of higher education under a royal "curator," where anyone might study or teach in greater freedom and which would better serve the interests of an intelligent citizenry. The desire to popularize knowledge and to make it the possession of a wider public than that to whom universities gave access was perhaps Engel's chief motive.

The plan came to rest in the archives of the Prussian ministry, and perhaps that was well. The center of popular learning which Engel proposed would quite likely have turned into a sort of Chautauqua. Then, too, the variety of individual character and achievement which the German universities in the different regions and provinces of the country were to reveal in the future would have been destroyed had higher education been centralized in the capital. Still, Engel's document was important because it added to the dissatisfaction with the existing academic conditions and to the desire for reform.

One might have supposed that Frederick the Great (1740–1786), in whose reign the Berlin Enlightenment began and who far exceeded his father in learning, good taste, and respect for intellectual interests, would have done something to initiate the reform of the universities. His opinion of them was as low as Engel's. True, he reinstated Christian Wolf in Halle with honors, and he admired men like Leibniz and Thomasius. Only these seemed to him rare exceptions in Germany. German erudition as a whole appalled him, just as he remained indifferent to German literature. When, in the first years of his reign and before his long and costly military campaigns, he attempted to raise the cultural level of Prussia, it was the Academy in Berlin, which he enlarged and reorganized as the Académie des Sciences et Belles-Lettres in 1744, and not the provincial universities to which he resorted. He invited famous foreigners, and especially Frenchmen, to become members of the Academy. But on the whole Frederick's attempt to infuse elements of Ancien Régime culture into backward Prussia was not successful. When the revival of German intellectual and literary life did come, it was inspired and quickened by the ideals of the French Revolution which Frederick did not live to see. But at the same time the revival drew its real strength from indigenous resources.

As long as absolutism remained—enlightened though it might be—education continued to be regarded as a branch of statecraft. As late as 1797 and 1804 general outlines of systems of state education appeared, treating education frankly as an affair of state and viewing the citizenry as instruments for the achievement of political and economic aims as prescribed by the king and the higher bureaucracy.[6] The individual with rights and personal aspirations, including the free development of his native powers, was not recognized. It was only the useful citizen, to be fitted into the existing social order with its established classes and corresponding occupations, who received the attention of the functional-minded bureaucrats. To their way of thinking, each class and occupation rendered the state distinct services, and accordingly a system of state education should be so organized as to maintain this social order and, if possible, to increase the efficiency of all its parts.

The absence of human freedom, which had been felt less acutely under Frederick the Great who was tolerant at least in religious and intellectual matters, became oppressive in the years following his death. In 1788 a royal edict sharply restricted the freedom of teaching and publication, and established an official inquisitorial committee to examine the orthodoxy and reliability of future Protestant preachers and schoolteachers. It was by authority of this edict that Immanuel Kant was severely reprimanded in 1794 for having violated his responsibility to Prussian academic youth and his duty to the crown. He was charged with having used his philosophy "for the purpose of distorting and deprecating several basic teachings of the Holy Bible and of Christianity." In the reprimanding letter the Prussian Minister Wöllner, who was also the author of the edict and showed not the slightest respect for the freedom of philosophical inquiry, ordered Kant to use his "prestige and talent for the realization of our Patriarchal intentions." [7] This recurrent and excessive interference of the absolutist state in affairs religious and intellectual, occurring at the time the French Revolution was taking place, created in many German intellectuals a deep hostility against state power.

When the break with the absolute state in Germany finally came, it found as passionate and dramatic expressions in German literature as it had in the writings of Rousseau. The radical alternative stated in the first pages of *Emile* that "you must make your choice between the man and the citizen, you cannot train both," was accepted in Germany. Humboldt and Goethe, who were among the earliest exponents of the new humanism, proclaimed the cultivation of human individuality as the supreme aim of education. In the novel *Wilhelm Meisters Lehrjahre* (1795–1796), perhaps the most popular and representative expression of this new aspiration, the hero is a young man of the well-to-do middle class who has rebelled against the social status assigned to him by birth. While traveling, he receives a letter from home urging him to return in order to assume responsibility for the family business, and he replies with youthful defiance: "What good will it do me to manufacture good iron as long as my own soul is full of dross, and to put a farm in order if I am in discord with myself?" He refuses to do what is expected of him, because to acquiesce in the utilitarian function which the existing class society prescribes for him would, in his opinion, dehumanize his life. What the young Meister most deeply resents is that he should be denied the right and the pleasure to develop his personality as he desires, and that instead his worth should be estimated solely in terms of what useful knowledge, skill, and industry he might put at the disposal of society. "It is assumed," he complains with bitterness over the fate of a man of his social status, "that there is not, nor is there allowed to be, any harmony in his character, because to become useful he must neglect everything else." [8]

The conception of life described by Goethe in his novel found expression also in contemporary German philosophy. Kant thought that men cannot achieve the dignity of rational beings as long as they use themselves, or one another, as means to the pursuit of material and selfish ends. In the new humanism of Goethe and Humboldt the development of the individual's moral and esthetic capacities and the free association of individuals, respecting freedom in themselves as they respect it in others, became the cardinal values. This humanistic ideal inspired all of classical German literature. It also produced the first basic German inquiry into the political conditions necessary for the realization of this ideal. The author of this inquiry was Wilhelm von Humboldt, in whom the new humanism found its finest expression. His essay on *The Sphere and Duties of Government* [9] is one of the few great documents of liberalism in the history of German political and educational literature. In the nineteenth century it inspired John Stuart

Mill in the writing of his famous essay *On Liberty*. Humboldt's hostility to the state was deep and his liberalism was radical. But unlike Count Mirabeau, whose writings helped to shape his early thought, Humboldt was radical only in thought. He never incited to revolution and his essay contains not a single expression of hatred nor a single inflammatory statement. His temperament and his philosophy made him shun extremes of action and emotion. He ultimately shared with Goethe the desire for harmony and wholeness which included a balanced and organic relationship between individual and society.

Humboldt's criticism of absolute monarchy, as set forth in his essay, was that by treating its citizens as mere instruments with which to obtain national power, prosperity, and efficiency, it thwarted the development of human individuality in its full, natural variety and the free association of human beings among themselves. He found himself in sympathy with Mirabeau's condemnation of the "rage of governing" and the excessive interference with the private lives of the citizens. But it was largely with ideas familiar from the educational philosophy of Rousseau that he developed the positive part of his liberalism. He pointed out how pernicious it was for the individual citizen habitually to rely upon state welfare and state services; how such reliance gradually destroyed his independence, his resourcefulness, his spontaneous sympathy and helpfulness toward his fellows. With this increasing passivity Humboldt feared men's energies and powers would atrophy in proportion as the state's services multiplied. When he said this, however, he was not thinking primarily of the economic activities of man, and he did not mean to present a brief for economic liberalism. He was pleading for a form of social organization which would allow complete freedom for the self-activity of the mind, for the growth of indigenous interests, for the expression of genuine tastes and beliefs, and for the formation of sincere and intimate relationships between human beings. Still, his liberalism would be more valid today had he made it clear that economic security, which inevitably involves some amount of external regulation and control, is a condition upon which the freedoms in which he was interested depend.

Humboldt did not deny that absolutism might prove beneficent and that it might actually concern itself with the intellectual improvement of its citizens. Yet he observed that in matters of education the state could do no more than determine the external, measurable results and standards to be achieved by its schools and universities. It was incapable of acting upon man's inner motives and feelings. This conviction Humboldt shared with Pestalozzi, who said that the task of modern education was not to nationalize man, but rather to humanize the state. Humboldt feared that by prescribing definite standards and by providing a unified national educational system, the state was likely to do more harm than good to human beings. It would seduce them to conformity of opinion and monotony of aspiration which would make it difficult for them to discover their true vocations. By offering various incentives for the acquisition of privileges, prestige, power, and social approval, the state only alienated man from himself. Self-realization, Humboldt thought, was achieved only in the disinterested pursuit of whatever man's vocation happened to be. In this sense, he wrote, all men, even "peasants and craftsmen, could perhaps become artists, that is, people who love their work for its own sake and thereby cultivate their minds, ennoble their character and increase their happiness." [10]

To stop education from being debased to a branch of bureaucracy or engineering, Humboldt wanted the powers of the state reduced to those absolutely necessary to deal with problems of internal and external security. Education, for one, was to be exempt from all state interference. Humboldt would have agreed with the principle, as stated by John Stuart Mill, that the state should require education but not provide it; both liberals, however, realized that the education of the children of the poor constituted a special case.

When Humboldt became Prussian Secretary of Education in 1809, he found himself compelled, as will presently be shown, to modify parts of this theory of liberalism. His fundamental values, however, remained the same. He continued to hold an idea unorthodox in German political thought of the nineteenth century: that the existence of the national state was justified only if it served to enhance the moral capacities of the individual. "The highest ideal . . . of the coexistence of human beings," he wrote, "seems to me to consist in a union in which each strives to develop himself from his own inmost nature and for his own sake." [11]

This humanist philosophy of education could not help but give a new meaning to university teaching and study and to knowledge itself. To the humanist, knowledge obviously could not mean the acceptance of traditions and formulae no longer understood, nor the accumulation of unintegrated information, nor power in the Baconian sense of this word. Of sole importance to him was the active mind which, while engaged in inquiry, enhanced its capacity for understanding the self and the world, and which yielded the inquirer that intimate pleasure which is derived from the awareness of such enhancement. Humboldt quoted with approval the famous statement of Lessing: "It is not the truth which a man possesses, or assumes he possesses, but the honest labor spent in the pursuit of it that determines a man's worth." He himself wrote to Madame de Staël, "The aim of all scientific work is the enlargement of man's character." [12] This was how he judged all human interests and activities. The ultimate purpose of our existence, he wrote in his fragment on *The Theory of the Education of Man* (1793), is to convey through our own person and our achievements a conception of the genius of mankind. Humboldt realized that in scholarship and science specialization was necessary, but he emphasized that a humanist scholar whose pleasure was in the life of the mind saw general truths reflected in the results of even limited inquiries. What he warned against was the collection of information unrelated to man's broader conceptions and his imaginative construction of the world. "As soon as he deludes himself that knowledge does not depend on creative

imagination, but that it can, by extensive efforts, be put together mechanically, everything will be irrevocably lost." [13]
He believed it to be important that every scholar make an
effort at integrating his results with the rest of knowledge,
and that he freshen his grasp and deepen the perspective of his
particular problem by re-examining his position in relation to
the whole, even if he can have no more than an intuitive and
general idea of it.

While Humboldt thus anticipated certain dangers of nineteenth-century science and scholarship, he was more concerned
over the lack of freedom which prevented the liberal university
from coming into existence. Humboldt was direct witness to
the absolutist policy of authorizing and prescribing the truth:
as a young man he served in the courts of Berlin at the time when
they enforced the edict of 1788. Obviously irritated by this
reactionary measure, he wrote at that time an essay entitled
On Religion (1789), in which he examined the psychology of
religious dogmatism, showing how it impeded the free and
original inquiry so essential to the liberal university. The following lengthy passage illustrates once more his militant humanism:
"Doubts torment only the dogmatic believer, never the independent inquirer. The general difference between them is that
to the latter results are of far less importance than to the former.
For while the latter investigates, he is aware of the action and
the strength of his mind, and he feels that his own perfection
and happiness rest upon this very strength. Any doubts which
may arise from his inquiry concerning certain propositions
which he once believed to be true, do not oppress him. On the
contrary, he is glad that his power of reasoning has increased so
that he now perceives errors which before had escaped him.
The dogmatic believer, on the other hand, is interested only
in results, not in the method of their discovery. Doubts suggested by reason embarrass him because, contrary to the independent mind, he does not see in them new means to arrive at
the truth. He only feels deprived of his certainty and is left without further means of regaining it. The upshot of this reflection,

carried a step farther, is that it is not well to attribute too great an importance to any particular findings and to think that so-and-so many other truths and consequences depend upon them; for this easily causes investigations to stagnate. . . . This goes to show the general importance of intellectual freedom, and the harm that may be done by any restrictions imposed upon it." [14]

The indignity of precisely such restrictions, which he had suffered in his own person, seems to have been a reason for Kant's publishing, after the edict had been revoked, a little treatise entitled *The Strife of the Faculties* (1798). Kant there set forth an argument much like that of Humboldt just quoted, and did his part to develop and establish a new philosophy of higher education. By the title of his treatise, actually a collection of three separate papers, Kant referred to the fact that since the Middle Ages the professional schools, or "faculties," of a university had been regarded as higher, and the faculty of philosophy or liberal arts as lower, because it offered courses preparatory to professional training. This distinction had been maintained in the territorial universities of the seventeenth and eighteenth centuries when absolutist governments, interested only in practical values, had renewed the prestige of the higher faculties. For the same reason the philosophical faculty, which pursued non-professional, disinterested studies, had fallen into disrespect. Now it was against this extraneous standard of valuation that Kant protested. He argued that the spirit of free rational inquiry, which was best represented by philosophy, constituted the very essence of a university. In admitting that the state had a practical interest in the teaching of law, medicine, and theology, he pointed out that these faculties were obliged to abide by definite truths prescribed by the state. This fact clearly established their inferiority to the faculty of philosophy by all germane standards. Philosophy, Kant insisted, must remain free of any kind of control. Its function was, in his opinion, to act as the judge and critic of all beliefs and actions, and to constitute the public voice of reason without which, he said, "truth would not see the light of day." With this argument and no less by the effect of his own work in philosophy, Kant helped to establish respect for the *libertas philosophandi* and the intellectual autonomy of the universities.

* * *

In 1809 Humboldt accepted the position of Secretary of the Department of Education and Religion (Sektion des Kultus und des öffentlichen Unterrichts) in the Prussian Ministry of the Interior. He stayed in office less than a year, but during that time succeeded in establishing the University of Berlin, which began instruction in 1810. By both these actions he deviated from his earlier, radical social philosophy. Without modification the theoretical rigidity and utopian character of his liberalism would obviously have put it beyond realization. Prussia, as most other European national states, had even then developed systems of centralized bureaucratic administration which had come to stay. Humboldt would have remained pure theorist had he actually relied for the improvement of education in Prussia solely upon voluntary effort, as he originally had thought desirable. Yet it would be an error to think that in modifying his liberalism so as to transform it into a program of action, Humboldt surrendered his fundamental convictions. Even Friedrich Meinecke, who in a well-known book has measured the greatness of the leading Germans of the Goethe period by their ability to outgrow cosmopolitan and anti-nationalist ideas, was compelled to admit that Humboldt continued to remain loyal to his humanist and liberal ideas in 1810, and even after 1815 when the political reaction began.[15]

The broad aim which Humboldt pursued as Prussian Secretary of Education was to use state power to effect liberal policies. The defeat of the Prussian army by Napoleon in 1806 and the long occupation which followed raised unexpected questions concerning the survival of Prussian sovereignty, the means of national resistance against the invader and, in more excitable minds, the question of preserving German culture and language. With the centralized state machinery thrown into disorder and in large part defunct, even an absolutist on the throne could be persuaded to call upon the untapped resources of the individual citizens and to ask liberals to join his government. Patriotic and bolder sentiments than had ever been allowed before were encouraged among the people, and a sense of individual responsibility and initiative was awakened which the passive and docile subjects of the old state had not known. Thus, a brief opportunity offered itself to Stein and Humboldt to liberalize the state by a number of great reforms: self-government for the towns, emancipation of the serfs, and abolition of a system of education maintaining separate schools for separate classes and vocations. Of these the first succeeded best and the last, least.

A good example of how welcome the temporary eclipse of the old state was to German liberals is provided by Friedrich August Wolf (1759–1824). This outstanding German classical scholar, who taught at the University of Halle until it was closed by Napoleon in 1806, was one of the leaders of the humanist movement and a friend of Humboldt, who later appointed him to the new University of Berlin. Wolf had for some time taken an active interest in the reform of university education and in 1807 he submitted to the Prussian Ministry suggestions concerning a new university in Berlin.[16] He expressed the frank opinion that the previous Prussian politics of aggrandizement and power had only impoverished the country and that the state had sacrificed the happiness of generations of citizens to costly ambitions and illusions. Without being in the slightest lachrymose or inclined to the rhetorical patriotism which the Napoleonic occupation roused in numerous other Germans, Wolf termed the national misfortune a salutary event. He hoped that it would show Prussia the way to civilized living, and with Humboldt he believed that the state might yet, under the pressure of circumstances, be transformed into an agent of culture. He was convinced that had Prussia emerged victorious, the power and insolence of the military caste would have become unbearable, and the end result of victory would have been the gradual but certain decay of German culture. In the course of the nineteenth century, fewer and fewer scholars were as militant in their liberalism as was this classical scholar and assistant of Humboldt.

Similar ideas, if less radical, came from the theologian Schleiermacher, who also assisted Humboldt in the organization of the University of Berlin and who was appointed to its faculty. Schleiermacher in his essay *Some Occasional Thoughts on Universities* (1808) helped to define the task faced by the liberals in office. He too was convinced that the universities could not become institutions of liberal education unless the state relinquished its demands for the immediate usefulness of science and learning, and unless the numerous restrictions, interferences, and suspicions from which the older territorial universities had suffered were removed. He made it clear that science, scholarship, and learning had an ethics and a psychology of their own which bureaucratic administrators usually failed to understand. The task of the liberal in government, therefore, was first to teach respect and understanding of the nature of intellectual work and ultimately perhaps to establish a republic of learning within the boundaries of the national state.

For all their strong convictions, neither Humboldt nor Schleiermacher lacked political instinct. They knew that to incline the crown in their favor it was better to dwell upon the benefits which the state itself would derive from liberal reforms, than upon the conflicts existing between learning and politics. Greater intelligence and competence of its officials, as well as higher standards in the professions were unquestionably of interest and advantage to the state. All that had to be done to obtain these advantages, so the liberals pointed out, was to create the conditions under which free inquiry and disinterested study flourished. "The state," Humboldt accordingly wrote in one of his official papers, "must principally not demand anything from the university which would serve its purposes directly, but it should cherish the conviction that if the universities accomplish their ultimate aims, they will thereby also serve its purposes and from a much loftier point of view." The state, he urged, should support and respect "pure science and learning" because these often bore their richest fruit when they seemed farthest removed from all immediate practical demands. He held to his early idea that the universities should treat knowledge as something that was in flux, as something that had continually to be refined; and his liberal loyalties were in evidence in the admission, made while he was Secretary of Education, that the state "almost always obstructs the moment it interferes" in learning and education and that "without it we would be infinitely better off." And as if to make quite clear how his own work was distinguished from that of the ordinary bureaucrat inclined to "over-government," he wrote: "My main endeavor is only to establish simple norms and to adhere to them strictly in my actions; not to undertake many things but to act resolutely in those that I do. The rest I leave to nature, which requires but an impetus and a first direction." [17]

During his term of office Humboldt asked the king for authority to remove several restrictions imposed upon the Prussian universities in the previous century and still in force. Among them was an edict of Frederick the Great from the year 1749, forbidding Prussian students to attend foreign, that is, other German, universities. Humboldt was successful in having this restriction revoked in 1810. Another edict, also from the previous century, forbade Prussian professors to accept appointments at non-Prussian universities. This restriction had been imposed at the time of the founding of the University of Göttingen which had attracted professors from elsewhere. It seems, however, that the government had not been able to enforce it for long, and Humboldt, by inviting the best men he could find in all of the German states to join the faculty of the University of Berlin, removed also this vestige of territorial policy. His ambition, as he stated repeatedly to the king, was to create in Berlin an international university, an institution of which his Majesty and all Germans could be proud. He also asked that the censorship for scholarly, scientific, and literary works—newspapers were not included—be abolished, which was granted. He finally submitted a proposal which, had it been accepted by the crown, would have given the University of Berlin a permanent endowment and, with it, financial and possibly greater political independence from the state. But in this he did not succeed.

While a liberal progressive in these respects, Humboldt proved a conservative in others. For example, he did not agree with Engel that the universities were clannish institutions, and accordingly did not suggest that they be replaced by some vaguely conceived higher-than-university institution. He was opposed also to Massow's plan, previously mentioned, of dissolving the university into separate professional schools. "University" meant to Humboldt an institution from which "no branch of study should be excluded." In other words, he remained within the tradition of the medieval *studium generale*. It was a conception of the university which accorded well with his humanist philosophy of education. For he thought of the institution not as an aggregate of professional schools, but as a place of responsible self-education with a strong accent on universality.

In reality the German university remained an institution in which the great majority of students prepared for the professions of medicine, law, and theology just as they had done in the medieval universities. Utilitarian motives of study, therefore, were bound to prevail, and the question arises whether Humboldt in his effort to create a permanent home for humanism in German higher education would not have done better to break the medieval mold. Fichte, for example, as will be shown in the following chapter, and Schelling, too, were convinced that such a break was necessary. But generally speaking, men in Humboldt's period regarded ideas as more influential than material conditions in shaping the conduct of man, and therefore the questions of organization were for the time being not the most important. Two or three decades later, however, when the political reaction had resulted in the general disillusionment of German intellectuals, a more radical institutional reform of the universities than Humboldt had thought desirable was proposed. Gervinus, for example, complained about the *Brotstudenten* who only thought of their future positions and careers, and suggested—to my knowledge for the first time—the establishment of liberal arts colleges after the English and American models. He thought that only by separating these colleges from the universities, which might then devote themselves exclusively to professional training, would humanism be given a true chance.[18] Gervinus' proposal was never acted upon. But the problem of defending and protecting liberal education against the various forces threatening its extinction in later years continued to occupy a number of philosophers and educators in Germany, among them Friedrich Nietzsche and later, in the twentieth century, Max Scheler. It is the very problem which will be pursued further in these pages.

Having committed himself to continue professional training within the universities, Humboldt also conceded to the government an interest in the appointment of professors. In fact, he was inclined to give the state ministry exclusive right in this matter, which was an extreme concession for a liberal to make. Humboldt stated that academic freedom is not only threatened politically, from the outside, but by cliques and schools of dogmatic thought from within. Accordingly he argued, and Schleiermacher agreed with him, that it was inadvisable to leave the appointments of professors entirely to the universities. Patronage and, as Schleiermacher put it, "a spirit of petty intrigue" were notorious academic vices from which intelligent officials in the Education Ministries could be expected to be free. This was certainly true in the case of Humboldt himself, who appointed most of the faculty of the new University of Berlin, but used his great power in the best interest of the institution. It was doubtful, however, that his understanding of university problems and his broad acquaintance with men of letters and science could be counted upon in his successors in office. As a matter of fact, it was Schleiermacher's, not Humboldt's, recommendation concerning the method of appointments which finally became the established practice in the

German states in the second part of the nineteenth century. An under-secretary in the State Ministry of Education received the nominations of three candidates from the department of the university in which the vacancy occurred, and he appointed one of these.[19]

When the balance of Humboldt's liberal reforms is drawn, it is necessary to remember that the fortunes of the German universities continued to depend upon the good will and the favor of the governments. The institutions were not in a position to insist upon any rights for there existed no constitution guaranteeing academic freedoms. Prussia in this respect remained more backward than some of the south German states which received constitutions in the years immediately after the Congress of Vienna. But even in the constitutional monarchies, academic freedom suffered infringements and violations until after 1850. It must also be remembered that the universities depended for their financial support largely upon state, and in some later cases upon communal, appropriations. There existed no large private fortunes from which institutions of higher education could have been endowed.

During the brief period between 1807 and 1815, the relations between the state and the universities in Prussia improved. Frederick William III even promised a constitution once the war against Napoleon was concluded. As evidence for his particular interest in the reform of Prussian education, nationalist German historians have been fond of quoting a phrase which the monarch is alleged to have uttered at a time when the future of his sovereign state had become most uncertain: "The state," he said to a delegation of professors from the University of Halle which Napoleon had closed, "must replace what it has lost physically by moral and intellectual powers." [20] But it is improbable that even in the midst of hard times the monarch felt any sympathy for liberalism. It soon became evident—as it did in Russia after 1812 under Alexander I—that whatever concessions to liberalism and popular patriotism had been made under stress, proved sources of grave danger to the maintenance of absolute monarchy. The latter, clinging to the theory of the divine right of kings and erecting the artifice of the Holy Alliance, tried in Prussia, Russia, and Austria to resist all modification. By borrowing a certain brand of Christian mysticism for its support, absolutism became in the nineteenth century even more reactionary and less enlightened than it had been under Frederick the Great. With fear dominating the crown and government of Prussia, it was no surprise that the political reaction began almost as soon as the military campaigns against Napoleon were over.

Many students returned from the war with a new sense of their own importance and with greater, if vague, desires for liberty. The experience of the war had also taught them to forget their provincialism and their regionalism, and to feel themselves citizens of a united nation of Germans. But since the nation of which they dreamed did not yet exist, the students began to form organizations and fraternities to help bring it into being. This was the origin of the *Burschenschaften*, the first of which was formed at the University of Jena in 1815, soon followed by others at other German universities. For the most part, the members of these organizations remained political romanticists who took pleasure in creating for themselves "old German" garb and manners, of cultivating German song, and of sporting long hair and beards. They had some influence in temporarily reforming and refining German student life. Their liberal ideals, however, were greatly restrained by their Teutonic patriotism, and, generally speaking, the twin popular political desires of that period, national unity and constitutional liberties, were not well matched for the promotion of radical political action. There were, however, some young radicals. At the Universities of Giessen and Jena, Karl Follen, a young instructor and a true revolutionary, led a small group of "Unconditionals" who demanded the removal, by any means, of princes and dynasties as necessary for the establishment of a German "moral republic" after the Jacobin pattern.[21] One of Follen's followers was Karl Ludwig Sand, a student of Protestant theology who, in 1819, committed the murder of Kotzebue which helped to precipitate the extreme reactionary measures against the universities in Prussia.

Students and universities had been politically suspect since 1817 when the representatives of the *Burschenschaften* from various parts of Germany met on the Wartburg, in the Grand Duchy of Saxe-Weimar, in order to unite in a national students' organization. The meeting was a festive and romantic affair and resulted in no political resolutions or programs. Nevertheless, the Prussian and Austrian governments believed that a vast revolutionary plot was in the making. The fact that the students threw a few books of "un-German" authors, including a Prussian police code, into a bonfire was regarded in Berlin and Vienna as gross insubordination and as the foreboding of revolutionary chaos. After that the Prussian government began to watch carefully over its universities and to restrict academic freedom. The rector of the University of Berlin, for example, was asked to name all the students who had taken part in the Wartburg celebration. Jahn, a zealous, rather raw Teutonic patriot who was perhaps the main inspirer of the new student movement, had to discontinue his lectures on German folklore at the University of Berlin, as well as the physical exercises which he, "the father of German gymnastics," conducted with many students in a field near Berlin. He was soon afterwards arrested. Schleiermacher, who was known to be a friend of the students and who did not conceal his contempt for the unfolding reactionary maneuvers, was compelled to cancel his course on politics at the University of Berlin. The police also spied on the sermons he delivered in one of the Berlin churches. Ernst Moritz Arndt, the friend of Minister Stein who joined the faculty of the new Prussian University of Bonn, established in 1818, was severely reprimanded for publishing demands for a constitution, freedom of the press, and freedom from the Prussian secret police which was beginning to spread its net all over the country. He too was soon arrested. A professor of theology at the University of Berlin was dismissed in 1819 without trial for having said in a private letter to the mother of Sand that the murder committed by her son was excusable because of the purity of the young man's convictions. The rectors and academic senates of the Universities of Bonn and Berlin protested courageously against these arbitrary interferences with academic freedom. They insisted that a university could not isolate itself from the discussion and clarification of problems of general social importance, and they pointed out that to interfere with the freedom of teaching and publication was to destroy the moral value of the universities. These protests, however, were in vain, and the very policy which Humboldt had condemned was now restored as the official policy of the Department of Education.

Relations between the government and the universities came to a full crisis in 1819, a few months after the murder of Kotzebue. Metternich invited the governments of the larger German states to Karlsbad in order to take joint measures against what he alleged to be a general anarchistic conspiracy. The meeting resulted in the Karlsbad Resolutions which urged the individual German states, among other things, to maintain a strict censorship of the press and of academic teaching; to establish a system of curators for the supervision of schools and universities; to suppress students' organizations and to establish a central commission at Mainz to spy out revolutionary activities. Prussia and Austria, which had thus far refused to grant constitutions and accordingly were most afraid of revolutionary activities, carried these resolutions out at once, Prussia becoming the more reactionary of the two. Certain German states, Württemberg for example, proved lax in applying the Resolutions, but still these succeeded in causing bitterness and disillusionment everywhere. The constant spying on, and policing of, the universities poisoned the intellectual atmosphere and the relationship between students and teachers. The physiognomy of the University of Berlin changed completely in less than a decade after it first opened amid great enthusiasm and anticipation. The Karlsbad Resolutions remained in force until the revolution of 1848. During these decades students and professors were persecuted, imprisoned, and a number of them fled abroad. But the vast revolutionary plot which the reactionary regimes had alleged to exist was never uncovered.

It was in the early period of the Reaction that the Prussian ministry made two appointments at the University of Berlin— that of Hegel in philosophy in 1818, and Ranke in history in 1825—which had broad political and intellectual significance. The Prussian ministry believed that in the philosophy of Hegel and in the historical interest of Ranke it had found two stabilizing forces which it could use for its own political purposes. The Minister Altenstein, in recommending Hegel for the chair left vacant since Fichte's death, assured King Frederick William III that the philosopher would mind his own business and refrain from participating in the political agitation of the day. He described Hegel's philosophy as moderate and "scientific." [22]

Hegel did not disappoint the minister's great expectations. Contrary to Schleiermacher, he was not close to academic youth, expressed no sympathy with its republicanism but spoke with disapproval of "the vanity of wanting to know everything better." His *Philosophy of History* and his *Philosophy of Law* were notable for the important role they attributed to the Idea, to Reason, and to the necessity of the dialectical process, which left little room for the freedom and responsibility of the individual man who had begun to stir in Germany since the Napoleonic Wars. Yet it is doubtful whether Hegel, as is often alleged, glorified the state and the established order of things. If one accepts his dialectic of history as the crucial element in his thought, his is clearly a philosophy of change in which the existing state and any supporting political theory can have no permanent status. Those who are inclined to condemn Hegel as the leading Prussian reactionary should remember also that in 1840 Schelling and Stahl were called to Berlin by Frederick William IV in order to restrain and uproot the "pernicious seed" of Hegelian rationalism. By that time the Hegelian "Left" had developed, causing considerable anxiety to the throne; for the

Hegelian Left drew precisely the conclusion that the existing social order was not rationally defensible.

Leopold von Ranke, who began his career as a teacher of history at the Gymnasium of Frankfort-on-the-Oder, attracted the attention of the Prussian ministry when he submitted his first study, *History of the Romanic and Germanic Nations* (1824), to the board of censors in Berlin, one of whom, Kamptz, was a zealot of the political reaction. This Prussian official had persuaded himself that the current "folly of republicanism" was caused in part by the teaching of ancient history in the secondary schools, because it filled the boys' heads with anachronistic ideas of ancient liberties. He thought that the study of modern history, which to him was the history of modern national states, should be encouraged in the universities, and accordingly he recommended Ranke, who showed great promise in that direction, to Minister Altenstein. The following year, in 1825, Ranke joined the faculty of the University of Berlin.

Ranke's appointment, too, bore fruit, but in a manner more subtle and less direct than the political design which had inspired it. In contrast to later nineteenth-century "political" historians, such as Haeusser, Droysen, Sybel, and Treitschke, Ranke neither as author nor teacher abused history as a school of patriotism. It is true he was a conservative and a royalist, but these political preferences he did not intrude into his writing or his teaching. His interest, as he had said in the preface to his first work, was only to relate things as they had actually occurred, to refrain from theorizing of all kind, but to establish historiography on the firm basis of the critical knowledge of its sources. Still, Ranke admitted that there *was* a relation between history and the politics of the time. In his autobiographical notes he said that the period of the Restoration was of greatest importance for the development of the historical studies.[23] Was it equally true to say that the study of history, as he conceived it, lent support to the Restoration, or Reaction?

Ranke answered this question in an address delivered at the University of Berlin in 1836. In discussing the relation of politics to history, he recommended the study of the latter as "paving the way for sane politics and for dispelling the obscurities and deceptions which in our time dance before the eyes of even the best men." [24] History, he said in open criticism of French rationalist and republican "utopias," contradicts the belief that all nations should be modeled alike according to some ideal constitution. History rather demonstrates the individuality of national life and development. Intimate familiarity with, and sympathetic understanding of, such individual growth is a requisite for all who plan to devote themselves to a political career. The chief mark of the statesman is *bürgerliche Klugheit*, a prudent conservatism which will seek to preserve, cultivate, and only gradually to perfect what it has inherited. The same view of the value of history was expressed by Ranke in the *Politisch-Historische Zeitschrift* (1832–1836) of which he was the editor. In the foreword to this journal devoted to the analysis of contemporary history, he wrote that political theorizing had so gained the upper hand that "rarely is an enterprise or an institution examined according to its own conditions." Here was a valuation of history which, while it ministered to the established order of things with arguments reminiscent of Burke's maxim that we should follow events, not lead or force them, seemed at the same time perfectly compatible with the view that history was impartial *Wissenschaft*.

Leaving aside, however, his belief in these pedagogical-political values of history, Ranke was, as far as historiography itself is concerned, truly impartial and loyal to his famous theory of recording nothing but *wie es eigentlich gewesen*. It is for this that he has been celebrated, for example by Lord Acton, as the outstanding leader of critical and empirical German historiography. Ranke stood in the midst of the great struggle between the speculative and the empirical methods which began in Germany in the 1820's, and the weight of his achievements and prestige helped to decide this struggle in favor of empiricism. As a historian, he was of course most sensitive to the *a priori* constructions of world history as undertaken by Hegel, his more famous colleague in whom he sensed his real antagonist. "All of Germany agrees and is full of fear over the harmful influence of a sophistic and empty philosophy which controls, or attempts to control, our university and whose sole effect lies in the spell of its strange formulas," Ranke wrote in 1827.[25] But he was not misled into an unqualified hatred of philosophy. He rejected philosophy only in so far as it attempted "to derive boldly from an insignificant and superficial knowledge . . . forced conclusions." [26] Nor was Ranke, in his attempt to define "the distinction between the historical and the philosophical school," driven into a primitive empiricism. Many later scholars misunderstood Ranke's frequently quoted "objectivity" as implying that philosophical conceptions were wholly irrelevant to the study of history. By this misunderstanding they helped in the deformation of the humanities which gave rise, later in the nineteenth century, to the cry over "the meaninglessness of *Wissenschaft*," of which more will be said in other chapters of this book.

Ranke himself had, in fact, a philosophy of history. In addition to the organic, anti-rationalistic view already referred to, he revealed it in the choice of his material: the great part of his work was devoted to the political growth of modern European states, and to the political conflicts through which they had evolved. He further expressed it in his conception of world history as a drama and as primarily an esthetic phenomenon, a view which a number of his critics found wanting in moral earnestness. Besides, Ranke thought that through the genius of individual nations certain ideas struggled for realization and perfection, a theory more Hegelian than one would have expected from him. Ranke would have added, of course, that the great drama, divinely inspired as he thought it to be, remained a drama of human impulses and struggles not reducible to any single formula or hypothesis. He believed, in deist fashion, that there was a plan and order in history; he was equally certain that the historian cannot demonstrate it, but can only lead men to "divine" it.

Obviously Ranke was far removed from the common type of

empiricist, and more than that, he recognized its menace even at his time. "This colossal race," he wrote of the Germans, as Jacob Burckhardt and Friedrich Nietzsche were again to write, only more acidly, "works all the harder at a thing the more insignificant it is." Ranke himself wrote a lucid prose, and he criticized his colleagues for not producing more readable histories. He advised one of his brothers who lacked his universality not to waste his time upon "that unfortunate Cornelius Nepos about whom . . . it is not worth learning anything because he is one of the most insignificant of Latin authors." [27] Whatever justice exists in the criticism of Yorck von Wartenburg, "Ranke ist ein grosses Okular" for whom historical personages remain actors on the world stage but do not become real as extensions of ourselves, it cannot be denied that his mind was moved by a strong humanistic interest. "Don't you agree," he wrote in one of his letters, "that the real interest we take in the external world is in seeking to transmute it into our inner individual possession?" [28]

However, it was not Ranke's humanism, which was just an echo of the previous period, but his empiricism which German academic men admired and imitated. It was history as research, not history as a liberal education, to which Ranke gave great impetus; and together with such scholars as Niebuhr, Savigny, and Böckh, he helped to transform the universities into research institutes in which the teaching and the study of the humanities as Humboldt had defined them fell into neglect. Universities henceforth took their pride in training new generations of specialists willing to devote themselves to limited tasks with a single mind. This revolution in the idea and the function of the university was on the whole a silent one—the open clash between experimentalists and idealists, described in the following chapter, excepted. Apprehensions and mild protests there were, as has already been indicated in connection with Gervinus. But the more vehement protest against this deformation of German higher education—for such it appeared to humanist eyes—was not forthcoming until Nietzsche. It was a silent revolution because the sense of educational responsibility on the part of the majority of academic teachers grew fainter and fainter. Men like Humboldt and Wolf, Fichte and Schleiermacher, who had revitalized the institution at a difficult moment in its history continued to be ceremoniously commemorated in academic addresses, but their educational ideals became alien in a period very differently preoccupied. Had this preoccupation been less exclusive, there need not have been so sharp a break with the spirit of the reformers. To know more and to know more accurately, to generalize more cautiously and to insist upon a knowledge of original sources obviously meant progress; and with this no educator had any reason to quarrel. The failure lay in not adjusting university teaching, the organization of knowledge and of courses so as to compensate for the increasing specialization and absorption in research. The fact was that research led teaching, as is evident from the German practice of allowing professors to offer courses on specific subjects in which their current research happened to engage them.

Yet no explanation of the decline of liberal education should seek all the reasons on one side. The easy victory of the empirical and experimental interests and modes of thought was made possible by certain prejudices and defects of the humanists and idealists themselves. These men had generally not distinguished clearly between ethical postulates and objective fact analysis. There is no question but that both the new historical scholarship and the method of experimental inquiry achieved great progress by merely distinguishing more sharply between what is and what ought to be. But this unquestionable progress in positive knowledge evoked in many minds the impression that humanism and idealism were obsolete philosophies which need no longer concern academic teachers, scholars, and scientists. The following chapter will discuss in some detail the strong feeling of contempt for German Idealism held by the pioneers of German experimental science. At this point an explanation is necessary of why humanism also, after its all too brief flowering, came into conflict with empiricism.

One of the characteristics of the humanistic movement was its outspoken partiality for classical antiquity. Both Wolf and Humboldt believed that the only way in which modern German youth could be humanized was through the study of the language, literature, and philosophy of classical Greece. They felt that there alone had human individuality achieved its greatest perfection. This belief they shared with many of their contemporaries, and numerous expressions of it may be found in the German literature and poetry of the time. That the interest of these humanists was not antiquarian, but esthetic and pedagogical is evident from the friendly relations which both Humboldt and Wolf had with the leading literary men of Germany. Wolf, for instance, dedicated one of his works to Goethe, whom he regarded as the finest example of the type of man which their humanist education strove to produce.[29]

Despite these broader interests and despite its communion with the ideal aspirations of the time, humanism was inevitably narrowed by its identification with the study of one particular branch of knowledge. A still more serious defect was its idealization of Greece. With this the humanists exposed themselves to the criticism of all those scholars who, in the course of the nineteenth century, restored a far more accurate, full, and realistic picture of antiquity to which the idealized version fell victim in a short time. Actually this idealization was largely a historical projection of the humanists' *own* high esteem of the value of human individuality, and there was no need of their attempting to establish it upon the shifting ground of historical evidence. It took some time for German educational thought to realize that the validity of an educational ideal cannot be established in that manner (the discussion of Max Weber in the last chapter will once more revert to this problem). By attempting it, the humanists merely caused an unnecessary and groundless conflict between a moral postulate and empirical historical study. Humboldt himself, it may be added, did not hesitate to designate as "un-Greek" such men as Aristotle and Euripides because they did not fit his conception of Greece.[30]

Yet, even if classical humanism had been less vulnerable, its esthetic and pedagogical interests would have yielded to the general urge to inquire and to explore which transformed all branches of knowledge into scientific or scholarly disciplines. The classics already turned their back upon Humboldt's conception of study with August Böckh (1785–1867), a student of Wolf. During the fifty-six years which he taught at the University of Berlin, Böckh occupied a position in the classics comparable to that of Ranke in history. His sole interest was in the empirical reconstruction of antiquity, not in its educational values. In the work on which his scholarly reputation rests, *The Public Economy of the Athenians* (1817), he warned that the ancient Greeks were not wiser or better men than ourselves and that, in fact, they were much unhappier than has commonly been supposed. It is also significant that Böckh inquired into a part of classical civilization, namely, its economic life and especially its system of finance, in which the humanists showed no interest.

* * *

The hopes that the political reaction which had begun in 1816 would at last end through the efforts of the Frankfurt Parliament of 1848 were disappointed. In fact, the revolutions of the same year were followed by reprisals and renewed repression by which the governments of several German states hoped to eliminate "the democratic filth from the German constitutions," to quote Frederick William IV of Prussia. The constitution which this monarch "imposed" upon Prussia in 1850 in no sense assuaged the bitter and wounded feelings. Furthermore, the universities continued to suffer from arbitrary government interferences. Dismissals of professors for political reasons were still common in the 1850's in Prussia as well as in other German states. The historian Theodor Mommsen and two of his colleagues were expelled from the University of Leipzig in 1851 for their liberal sympathies. In other universities church orthodoxy, which had formed an intimate alliance with reactionary governments, was responsible for violations of academic freedom: David

Friedrich Strauss was dismissed from Tübingen, and Moleschott and Kuno Fischer from Heidelberg, Fischer for nothing worse than a mild "pantheism" which had given offense to his colleagues in theology. The decade of the 1850's was the last period in which Protestant orthodoxy was successful in suppressing rational thought and critical scholarship in a number of German universities.[31] The Catholic Church, on the other hand, was a powerful reactionary force still in 1870, but its punitive measures were at that time restricted to professors of Catholic theology who refused to accept the dogma of papal infallibility.

When the last reactionary wave had spent itself, the liberalism of most German intellectuals and university professors had grown feeble. The term "liberalism" remained in the German political vocabulary, but it began to assume a new, strange meaning in the 1860's. When, in 1848, it became apparent that national unity was not to be achieved through the voluntary federation of the German states, including Austria, the only alternative of real promise seemed to many to be the expanding power of Prussia which, by means of force, might establish its hegemony over the remaining German states. Before Bismarck gave the policy of Prussia this direction, a number of German professors of history and politics undertook to prepare German public opinion for its acceptance. The best known of these included Mommsen, Haeusser, Sybel, Droysen, and Treitschke. The peculiar form of "national liberalism" by which the politics of these professors became known was characterized by their outspoken anti-Hapsburg, anti-French, and anti-Catholic, as well as by their pro-Prussian, pro-Hohenzolleren, and pro-Protestant feelings. If any of them still deserved the epithet "liberal" in even a limited sense, it was Mommsen, in whose contradictory character there was loyalty to the ideal of intellectual freedom as well as enthusiasm for a Prussian Germany. The Prussian government so little feared his political radicalism that after his dismissal from the University of Leipzig, it appointed him professor at the University of Breslau in 1854 and later at the University of Berlin. Yet while in Prussian service Mommsen retained more independence of opinion and integrity than the members of the Prussian school of history. Evidence of this is his attack on certain policies of Bismarck and his opposition to the anti-Semitism of the 1870's which, led by Treitschke among others, had begun to invade the universities.[32] On the other hand, Mommsen's famous *History of Rome* was written with Prussian nationalist bias. It was political history, the essence of which was conflict and war, and it expressed admiration for Caesarism and power politics. Mommsen is also a good illustration of the growing sense of national pride and self-sufficiency which took possession of so many German "liberals" after the successful wars against Denmark, Austria, and France. "We are not modest by any means and do not wish it to be thought of us," Mommsen said.[33]

Droysen, Sybel, and Treitschke, who became the best known members of the Prussian school of history, were more whole-hearted nationalists than Mommsen. They thought Ranke's "objectivity" anemic and felt no hesitation in expressing their convictions not only as political pamphleteers and journalists, but also as university lecturers. "The true academic policy," Sybel wrote as early as 1847, "is to penetrate every study with interest in public affairs and to keep in view its value for national concerns." Under the influence of their teaching— and their careers took them to both north and south German universities—history was deprived of the sense of humility with which Ranke had approached it. With them it ceased utterly to be a liberalizing influence and became instead the vehicle of narrow prejudices. With the help of these men nationalism added its force to the influences already at work in the narrowing and dehumanization of German higher education. While Ranke had still believed that *all* periods were "immediate to God," Sybel exclaimed, after Prussia's military victory over France, "What have we done that God's grace should allow us to witness such mighty things!" [34]

It is useful in taking the full measure of these men to compare them with some contemporaries who viewed and judged

history very differently. There were, for example, the so-called
cultural historians Wilhelm Dilthey and, especially, Jacob Burckhardt, who wrote the history of art, literature, and religion and
who, in their analysis of the individual's creation and appreciation of these values, gave once more a humanistic interpretation
of history. More will be said of this in the chapter on Nietzsche.
One may further compare them with Karl Marx in order to
illumine their lack of breadth and historic vision. Instructive,
finally, is a comparison with the political-minded professor of
the first half of the nineteenth century who was represented
in the Frankfurt Parliament, and especially by the famous
Göttinger Sieben.

The *Göttinger Sieben* was a group of professors who publicly
protested the arbitrary action of the King of Hanover in 1837,
revoking the constitution which had been granted by his prede-
cessor a few years earlier. Since neither state nor church officials
dared to join in the protest, the king easily branded the Seven
as traitors and expelled them from the University and the country. In exile—they soon found positions in the universities of
other German states—Dahlman and Jacob Grimm explained the
reason for their action. They said that by acquiescing in a
lawless act, they would have lost their own integrity, and as
teachers of youth would have set an example of immorality.
They regarded the university as the conscience of the country,
and though, as Grimm explained, scholarship was their devotion, moral courage was in times of stress the first requisite
for a professor. Teaching, to have any positive influence, supposed mutual respect between teacher and student. Since the
government had made such a relationship impossible, the Seven
preferred to leave the country as honest men.[35]

The political-minded professors of the latter part of the nineteenth century showed no such moral sensitivity when similar
issues came before them. A case in point is Treitschke's response
to Bismarck's "editing" of the Ems Telegram in 1870. Bismarck's
misrepresentation of this French diplomatic communication in
the German press aroused German national indignation over

French "impudence" and made further negotiations for peace between France and Prussia difficult, if not impossible. Treitschke, who had been in a state of great excitement during the weeks immediately preceding the war, feared that the Prussian king might oppose Bismarck's desires and refuse to go to war. But when he read Bismarck's edition of the French note, he was jubilant. "What a humiliation we have escaped! Had not Bismarck so cleverly edited the telegram, the King would have given away again." [36]

To complete this characterization of the Prussian school of historians, a brief reference to their opposition to social reforms is necessary. The need for such reforms giving the working class a minimum of social security was urged not only by the political Left, but by certain university professors who were mockingly called "academic socialists" (*Kathedersozialisten*). These "socialists," among whom Gustav Schmoller at the University of Berlin and Lujo Brentano at the University of München showed the greatest concern for the social problem, were professors of economics and economic history who caused industrialists and nationalists considerable discomfort by inquiring into the working conditions of certain branches of industry and agriculture. Though they remained first and foremost men of *Wissenschaft*, they assumed the responsibility, in Schmoller's words, of "illumining practice by theory." Together with officials, journalists, and progressive manufacturers, they founded, in 1872, the *Verein für Sozialpolitik* which helped greatly to broaden public knowledge of social conditions and problems in Germany. Concerning economic doctrine, the academic socialists were equally as far removed from the economic liberalism of Adam Smith as from the communism of Karl Marx. They advocated a mild form of state socialism, on the principle that the state was responsible for a certain measure of social security for the masses. But Treitschke, Schmoller's colleague in Berlin, suspected them of anarchy and denounced them as partisans of the Social Democratic Party. He was as chauvinistic as he was reactionary. He asserted that the average working day cannot be much reduced, that there is "no culture without servants," and that it is "necessary to maintain an ignorant working class if the education of the higher classes is not to become impossible." [37] He held to these views until he died in 1896. That time had passed him by is evident from the fact that even Bismarck urged the social legislation of the 1880's because he realized, perhaps not wholly without Schmoller's influence, that economic liberalism had become unworkable.

CHAPTER II

THE IDEALIST CONCEPTION OF A UNIVERSITY

IDEALISM, rather than the humanism just described, has commonly been regarded the more characteristically national as well as the more consequential philosophy in Germany in the early nineteenth century. Whatever the truth of this general estimate, certain important differences exist between the two philosophies, differences which become especially marked when Humboldt as the representative of the one is contrasted with Fichte as the representative of the other. The educational aims of Fichte, which in this chapter are examined with special reference to the university, were the opposite of Humboldt's in that they required the socialization of the individual in a unified system of national state schools. Such a system is prone to result in a high degree of cultural uniformity and in inculcating in the individual absolute loyalty to the state. It has been made clear that there was nothing to which Humboldt was more opposed. There were differences also in temper and moral outlook. Fichte revealed a severe puritanical bent of mind which sought to justify human existence through a higher righteousness and by an effort to remake the world and man according to a rational order. His was an emphatically heroic ethics in which the will was indomitable and action involved the conquest of all resisting forces, including man's own sensual desires and moral apathy.

It was at the University of Jena shortly before 1800 that German Idealism began to have a reformatory influence upon academic study and teaching. There, in 1794, Fichte received a professorship, and there Schelling and Hegel too began their university careers. At the time the atmosphere of the University was charged with great expectations. The rumble of the French Revolution had been heard in the distance, and the great event created a general intellectual unrest which found expression in German literature even before it affected philosophy. Weimar, the capital of the tiny Duchy of Saxe-Weimar and the center of German literary life, was within a short distance of Jena, and this proximity helped to promote close relationships between poets and philosophers. Goethe, as a minister of the Duchy, had a hand in university appointments. Schiller had lectured on history at Jena in 1789, and there were numerous personal contacts and friendships between the literary men and the young Idealist philosophers. The latter became convinced that the great times demanded great things from them too, greater than were ordinarily accomplished in academic careers. They were enthusiastic and inspiring teachers and, during the short period which ended with the Napoleonic invasion in 1806, made Jena the most brilliant of German universities. In the course of their work, which they continued at other universities and especially in Berlin, they succeeded in establishing the importance of philosophy as the basis of a general education.

The young professors of philosophy conceived of their work as a mission. They thought they discovered among their contemporaries a new need for spiritual certainty which they were ambitious to satisfy. "The public," said Hegel, "comes to philosophy for the religion it has lost and only secondarily for knowledge. People want to know where they stand." [1] Schelling, in a significant fragment entitled *On the Nature of German Philosophy*, viewed the Idealists' mission in the light of German history. The medieval German mystics, he wrote, who broke away from the dogma of the Church were the first to express that profound intellectual unrest of the German mind which seeks certainty through individual reason and inquiry. Like them, Schelling believed, "a rebirth of religion based upon the highest kind of knowledge was the task which the German mind had to accomplish." [2] Fichte expressed the same conviction in almost Biblical language. Once man began to philosophize, he said, he lost his original innocence. "Ever since, man has philosophized because he had to, for want of redemption." [3]

The Idealists were aware that they carried German Protestantism to its conclusion. The motive now was to save one's soul by means of individual knowledge, and one may say that in their minds the university, whose "ministers" they became, assumed the importance of the church. Their rationalism resembled that of the Scholastics, but differed from it in the emancipation of philosophy from the position of merely justifying doctrinal and revealed truths. The Protestant philosophers followed nothing but their own conscience and their metaphysics was the rationalization of their individual faith and revelations. They rejected all authority, even, as Santayana has suggested, the authority of those whose experience and thought might have been deeper or broader than their own. For was not the receiver of alien acquisitions easily seduced into shallow conformity and mental passivity when the vital self-trust of the active mind was man's only hope?

The German Idealists' desire to find salvation through the effort of the mind gave the university a dignity which it had not possessed since the great period of Scholasticism. The scholar and professor were assigned the most eminent rank in the intellectual life of the country and great popular respect was created for their position and work. The Idealists' moral pathos spurred on research and scholarship, activities to which an increasing number of men dedicated themselves in the nineteenth century with a zeal and self-abnegation that bordered on the religious.

Among the Idealists it was above all Fichte who described in terms of the sublime and heroic the duties of the scholar in a series of popular lectures entitled *The Vocation of the Scholar*,[4] delivered in Jena on Sunday mornings in a university auditorium. Fichte used the term "scholar" in a far broader sense than is customary today. It was not the man devoted to erudition and pure research whom he extolled, but the man so possessed by an idea that he was relentlessly driven to communicate it to, and realize it in the lives of, his fellow men. Fichte's scholar resembled Plato's guardian in his single devotion to the public good, in the absolute negation of selfish and material interests in his own person, and in the capacity for constructive, speculative thought. These capacities the scholar had to have in order to make the sensual, egotistic mass of men, as well as the material world in which they live, conform to a rational order which he, first of all, had to discover. His responsibility was to make men understand that God intended their lives to have a meaning and purpose, and that they were not free to vegetate and to indulge themselves.

In these lectures Fichte asked his students to remember that university study was a privilege, given to a few, which imposed upon them extraordinary responsibilities. "The real self-abuse of men," he warned them, "lies in their degrading themselves to means for the obtainment of temporary and transient goods, and in their caring and laboring for anything which is not immutable or eternal." [5] He also reminded them that to work for the realization of the moral world order at a time when it continued to be violated by countless acts of individual greed and self-seeking pleasure required absolute incorruptibility on their part. The scholar, said Fichte, knows as well as anyone that ideals cannot be wholly embodied in this world. What distinguishes him from the lax multitude of men is his uncompromising stand: he insists on judging and modifying the existing world by his ideal. Such rigor and righteousness, he admitted, were likely to isolate the idealist from the crowd, and even to result in his persecution by the powers-that-be. But persecution held no threat for Fichte; it only caused him to show his true mettle. Persecution, he said, gives the scholar a great opportunity for setting a heroic example which teaches men far better than words can persuade them. By being loyal to the ideal in the moment of crisis, scholars become the salt of the earth. "I am called upon to testify for the truth," Fichte exclaimed with a sense for the dramatic. "My life and fate are of no importance, but the effects of my life are of infinite importance. I am a priest of the truth. . . . If I should be persecuted and hated for her sake, even if I should die in her service, what great thing would I have accomplished other than my ordinary duty?" [6]

Even in Fichte's own mind the moral law was not as immutable as his categorical manner of expression would lead one to suppose. In his youthful period, it was shaped by eighteenth-century rationalism and cosmopolitanism. Later, under the impact of the Napoleonic wars, Fichte's cosmopolitanism was attenuated, though not entirely extinguished, and the moral law became for him primarily a matter of devotion and loyalty to the Prussian state. In the *Patriotic Dialogues* (1807), the *Addresses to the German Nation* (1808), and the essay *On Machiavelli* (1813), Fichte's political and educational philosophy assumed the form of a national socialism.

With regard to the differences between German Idealism and humanism already alluded to, it is significant that, whereas Humboldt was admired by J. S. Mill, it was Carlyle who in the fifth of his lectures on *Heroes, Hero-Worship and the Heroic in History* (1840) paid tribute to Fichte and his idea of an adamantine elite. Oppressed by the fear of growing cultural mediocrity and materialism, Carlyle gave a violent affirmation of German Idealism. "The man of intellect at the top of affairs: this is the aim of all constitutions and revolutions, if they have any aim. For the man of the true intellect, as I assert and believe always, is the noble-hearted man withal, the true, just, human and valiant man." [7] He urged intellectuals to organize themselves so that their power of establishing cultural standards would be uncontested. As with Fichte, the eminence of such an elite rested upon their intuitive certainty of the divine idea to be realized on earth by themselves. "The hero is he who lives in the inward sphere of things, in the true, divine and eternal, which exists always, unseen to most, under the temporary, trivial." [8] Inequality among men was, therefore, natural

to Carlyle and hero worship seemed to him the chief means of
organizing and maintaining a society. New England tran-
scendentalism, too, showed many strains congenial to German
Protestant Idealism. There are, for example, in Emerson's
American Scholar (1837), phrases which could have been written by Fichte: "The only thing in the world of value is the
active soul," "There can be no scholar without the heroic mind,"
and "If the single man plant himself indomitably on his instincts
and there abide, the huge world will come around to him." Yet
Emerson was far more democratic than either Fichte or Carlyle.
He did not ask for a special intellectual elite, for the "scholar" to
him was merely "man thinking," and that might be any man.

Fichte's Lectures of 1794 were among the first expressions of
the new Idealist philosophy of education. Schelling, Steffens,
and Schiller contributed to its further development in Germany,
which was rapid during a decade of intense educational interest
and discussion.[9] When, in 1807, the Prussian Minister Beyme
asked a number of professors for ideas and suggestions concerning the reform of higher education, it was, however, again
Fichte who submitted the most extensive, detailed, and tightly
constructed plan of a university.[10] This plan constitutes the best
application of German Idealist philosophy to the practical
problems involved in the reorganization of higher education
which was being proposed at the time. The ideas set forth in
it were not exclusively Fichte's own. Schelling, especially, must
receive part of the credit for stating, in his Lectures in 1802, some
of the more important ones. Schelling stated that in order to
revitalize university education it was necessary to teach knowledge, not in the form of fixed results but as the history of its
genesis and gradual refinement. A university, he said, should
awaken young men's understanding of the interrelatedness and
the unity of knowledge; it should not cater to specialist, professional, and utilitarian interests. Philosophy he regarded as
the queen of the sciences because it taught the art of constructive, imaginative synthesis of all particular knowledge and information. Unfortunately, Schelling's mode of expression is,

in my opinion, so lacking in definiteness and clarity that it is often difficult to be certain of his meaning. Fichte, though not wholly exempt from this reproach, presents less of a problem to the ordinary intelligence. For this and the other reasons already stated, his plan has here been selected for an analysis and criticism of the major Idealist contributions to the theory and organization of higher education.

In what follows, the most important and suggestive of Fichte's ideas are presented and interpreted under six headings. The discussion of these ideas will attempt to illumine from various aspects Fichte's main thesis which is that a general education is obtained through the study of philosophy. Under the last, or sixth, heading the idea of an intellectual elite will be re-examined with particular reference to Fichte's nationalism.

(1) *To study philosophy is to raise thinking to the level of conscious artistry.* If man's progress in leading a rational life— for Fichte the only meaning of history—is to be assured, universities must develop and transmit a conscious understanding of the acts which constitute learning. Whenever the institutions have in the past been intellectually stagnant, this was, according to Fichte, because they failed to cultivate learning as an art. Instead of inquiring into what it is that men do when they learn, they have for too long given exclusive attention to subject matter which had simply to be memorized. Thus the powers of understanding were not developed as the constantly growing amount of knowledge required. Furthermore, in so far as an advancement of science and philosophy did take place, it was the result of accidental ingenuity and curiosity and remained wholly dependent upon the sporadic occurrence of natural interest and genius. To a thorough rationalist such as Fichte, it was intolerable and even humiliating that man should be satisfied to leave the possibility of his progress to the gifts of nature, that is, to forces beyond his control.

Therefore, Fichte was determined to give chief attention to how, rather than what, students learned. To be gifted with the power of clear observation, he remarked, might indeed be valuable in science, just as loving patience and sensitivity were valuable in the historical reconstruction of the past. But, and this is a recurrent and favorite thought of his, these faculties are only natural endowments and those who possess them are motivated as if by instinct. Unable to give even themselves a rational account of the purpose and method of their work and being scholars by a mere accident of nature, they would not know how to teach others. Now the men he wanted for teachers in his university must above all be able to show how an interest in science or history is consciously acquired and how learning is motivated by clear purpose. Those "naturals," Fichte admitted, might be assigned limited responsibilities, but in his university they would be of little use. They would not teach the basic courses, but might be available for special advanced work. Their place was in the academy of science which he planned to connect with the university. The question, then, is in what sort of courses and from what teachers would Fichte's students learn the art of thinking?

Fichte was convinced that before the student could engage in the study of a particular subject or branch of knowledge, he must have a clear conception of its value and its purpose, of the problems that await him and the methods which are employed to solve them. In this way all haphazard study and the confusion resulting from lack of direction would be avoided. The student was to be put in a position to make a deliberate and well planned effort at understanding and mastering any material, whatever its amount or complexity. That this might be achieved, all students in the first year would be enrolled in introductory courses which Fichte called "encyclopedias." For each major branch of knowledge one such encyclopedic course would be provided. Students would be required to pass not only the encyclopedia introducing them to the field of their choice, but all encyclopedic courses offered. Fichte's reason for insisting on such a broad theoretical foundation was to make students aware from the outset that the so-called branches of knowledge issue from but one stem. It was a precaution against an unimaginative specialism in the professions; and, he could have added, students so trained would be prevented from becoming the victims of meaningless "research." Generally speaking, these courses were to give students a sense of the importance, the fascination and distinction of intellectual life.

Fichte described the content of the encyclopedias in some detail. They were to define the characteristic differences in modes of thought that existed between the various fields. They were to describe which sciences were supplementary to each branch of learning and in what order the various subjects should be studied. They were to provide the student with the necessary literature and direct his reading. Only after having passed all the encyclopedias by written examinations at the end of the first year would a student be admitted into the "regular" student body. It is clear that Fichte thought of these courses as the foundation of academic instruction, and he knew that their success would depend upon finding teachers with sufficient intellectual vigor and breadth of knowledge. Since no such generation of teachers had yet been trained, Fichte proposed that they be trained in the projected institution.

For this purpose—and on the assumption that he would be called to organize the institution—he planned to conduct regularly a professors' seminar which would permit him to know his prospective teachers and to select from among them those whom he thought best fitted to teach the encyclopedias in the spirit he desired. He expected the professors' seminar to do for the teachers what the encyclopedias would do for the students. Through this central, controlled training institute Fichte hoped to preserve in all the departments of his university the unity of its chief purposes: making certain that all studies were carried on meaningfully and systematically; instilling in students and teachers alike a taste for disinterested thought and inquiry; making them aware of the unity of all knowledge by teaching them to regard it as an integrated system of meanings created by the human mind, without which nature is tragically incomplete. The unity of knowledge, as shown in the first chapter, was stressed by a number of contemporary writers on university reform, including Wilhelm von Humboldt and Schleiermacher. The Idealists even reinterpreted the word "university" itself as meaning universality and unity of learning, a meaning which had been familiar to the great Scholastics, though in the Middle Ages the idea was expressed by the term *studium generale* rather than by *universitas*. Among the Idealists, Fichte again had the clearest idea of that meaning, for in his *Plan* he suggested definite means for its realization.

In reviewing Fichte's program of general introductory courses, it should be stated that he realized both their dangers and the probable opposition they would encounter. He made light of the latter, saying that it would come from the professors who had themselves fallen victims to professionalism and departmentalism, and who would of course be embarrassed were they asked to present a systematic and comprehensive view of their subjects. As to the dangers, Fichte admitted that "to stop at such general surveys and results betrays shallowness, laziness, and a desire for cheap splendor." What he feared worse, however, was desultory and aimless study, and the drab, petty utilitarianism which is apt to overgrow a university when economic and technical needs are allowed to determine its offerings. It must be remembered that the supreme aim of Fichte's university was to transform conventional and irrational young men into exceptional and rational beings. And nearly as important was what he termed a "philosophic," and what we would call "general," education. The reader will already have discovered how relevant Fichte's ideas are to the contemporary movement to restore the American liberal arts college as a place of general education.

(2) *To teach in a philosophical spirit is to stimulate students to become creative thinkers.* At the beginning of his *Plan* Fichte said that universities ought to be denied further existence if their teaching continued to be no more than a duplication of the content of books. Mere information could obviously be obtained more reliably from them than from lecture notes. Only

on one condition did the academic lecture seem to him to continue to have a distinct value: if the lecturer avoided being an impersonal dispenser of dead "material," and instead, while preserving the form of the lecture, actually employed the art of the dialogue so as to both ask and answer questions which he himself first suggested to the students' minds. This ability of the teacher to communicate with the student in the common pursuit of an idea was to Fichte essential for all good teaching on university level. It required a ready knowledge of the genesis and gradual refinement of accepted truths, of relevant criticisms and arguments to be adduced in their support, and of their possible application. Creative teaching proceeded from and ended in the free, imaginative mind. Its aim was not to teach only what men knew already; it was to extend human understanding.

Seminars and examinations were further means to this end. Oral or written examinations, Fichte insisted, must never consist in parroting teachers' words, nor in merely checking upon the student's memory. They should be occasions for the student to show what he can do with what he has learned. They should be tests of the "self-activity" of his mind. Of course, to make up tests of this kind required imagination also on the part of the examiner. The professor of Roman law, Fichte illustrated, might give the student an imaginary case and ask him to suggest a law that could be derived from it and which would harmonize with Roman legal thought. The student's answer would demonstrate, said Fichte, whether he really knew Roman law in the sense that he understood its basic ideas, or whether he had merely memorized isolated facts. As for seminars, Fichte would prefer them to lecture courses wherever possible. They seemed to him the most effective method of teaching, and in fact he recommended that the Socratic dialogue be reintroduced. "Not only the teacher but also the pupil must continually express himself and communicate his thoughts, so that their mutual relationship may become a continuous conversation in which each statement by the teacher shall be the answer to some question asked by the pupil. . . . In this manner the teacher addresses not someone quite unknown, but one who continually reveals himself until the teacher completely penetrates his mind." [11]

With such aims and methods of teaching there can hardly be any quarrel. But it is difficult to follow Fichte further when, with the rationalist's belief in the nearly unlimited power of the conscious intellect, he asserted that the arts of thinking and learning could be perfected to a degree where they would infallibly lead to new discoveries and assure the triumph of uninterrupted originality. It is as if Fichte wanted to insure man against the limitations and vicissitudes of nature. But no rules have yet been found by means of which men can learn infallibly to ask significant new questions or even answer them.

(3) *Philosophy has a right to the free rational critique of the assumptions and principles of all other branches of learning.* With this proposition Fichte largely reiterated Kant's thesis developed in *The Strife of the Faculties*,[12] with which he may well have been familiar. He was convinced that the progress of *Wissenschaft*, by which he meant systematic inquiry and rational understanding, was retarded whenever knowledge was taught or appreciated for primarily practical purposes. Since this was the tradition, especially in the professional departments of law, medicine, and theology, it was important that in the reformed university these departments should be made to recognize their fundamental dependence on philosophy. Philosophy, according to the Idealists, least of all relied on tradition, authority, conventional practice, or experience. On the contrary, it established the criteria by which these might be revised, or even overthrown. By its power of reviewing and revolutionizing the theories of science and history, it was superior to all other branches of learning.

Fichte illustrated this proposition. For example, none other than the teachers of philosophy were to provide the teachers of law with the concept of right. In the interest of a philosophic and systematic study of law, students, who were the legal reformers and legislators of the future, should study as a basic course the philosophy of right. This course would offer "a history of the development and improvement of the concept of right among men" (§26). Concerning the teaching of medicine and science Fichte made a similar though less explicit suggestion. As regards Protestant theology, finally, he was positive that if it were to be taught at all, it must abandon its claim to dogmatic and revealed truth. For otherwise the university, whose very purpose was to educate men to a *rational* understanding of the world, would be deprived of its inner unity. Theology would accordingly be taught as the "history of the development of religious ideas among men," pagan peoples not excluded. It would form, together with the history of science and law, part of the subject matter of the introductory courses.

(4) *A university shall not assume the burden of professional training.* As his analysis proceeds, it becomes increasingly clear that Fichte was determined to break with the traditional organization of universities and to create in their place high schools of philosophy, or theoretical knowledge. Unlike Kant, Humboldt, and Schleiermacher, who possessed a stronger sense for historical continuity, Fichte planned to eliminate all courses designed exclusively to prepare the student for specific professional work. The practical training of judges, lawyers, pastors, physicians, and teachers was, in his opinion, the task of special institutes separate from the university and under the direction of experienced professional men and officers of the state. Fichte obviously felt that it was beneath the dignity of the university to be used for the maintenance of routine social services. But, more important, he feared that by shouldering this burden, university study would be so crowded by practical requirements and technical courses that the general theoretical disciplines would suffer progressive amputation and students' imaginations would be crushed by factual information. As educational developments since have shown, this fear was not unjustified.

(5) *Certainty of knowledge depends upon teaching a single system of philosophy.* According to Fichte's definition of philosophy as the art of thinking, one would assume that there was no necessity for his university to commit itself to the teaching of a single particular system of philosophy. Yet this is what

Fichte strangely insisted upon. "At the inception of this institution there must be only one philosopher; beside him, no other shall have an influence upon the development of the student's philosophical understanding" (§18). He seems to have been unaware that this demand contradicted the chief purpose of his plan, namely, to liberate young minds through the study of philosophy. No great progress can be made in this direction if students are kept ignorant of conflicting views. Fichte seems to have thought that one system was nearer the truth than another, and obviously he assumed that the system adopted by his institution would be of the more perfect kind. If this was his conviction, it was still the job of a philosophical education to help the students discover for themselves the fallacies of relativism and to discriminate between inferior and superior systems of thought. Yet Fichte seems to have been afraid of trusting young minds that far, and the reasons for that fear may have been twofold. The strong urge to reform and save the world made him an impatient man, inclined to intolerance, absorbed in the importance of his own ideas and thus illiberal in the sense of lacking fundamental freedom of attitude. He was further convinced that certainty concerning the ultimate problems and values of life was attainable only if the inquiry was carried on within a single system of philosophy (§18). One concludes that he naïvely mistook inner consistency for truth, and that any system to him demonstrated "scientific" validity, or made a legitimate claim to be *Wissenschaft* if it could be shown to be free of inner contradictions. The immaturity, the subjectivity and lack of humility inherent in such a philosophical position have been described by George Santayana with just, but deadly, irony in his *Egotism in German Philosophy*.

This subjective authoritarianism was not fundamentally alleviated by Fichte's provision that the philosopher of the university "must not proceed from his system, nor from any positive thesis, but only stimulate the students' systematic thinking" (§18). Reiterating the purpose stated earlier in his *Plan*, Fichte said that his aim was to train self-active minds. One is forced to object that their freedom extended no futher than the established system of the philosopher, who found it inconceivable that anyone should reach final conclusions different from his. If that happened, Fichte added with astonishing naïveté, "a mistake has been made somewhere" (§18). It is not unfair to Fichte to assume, as already remarked, that he himself hoped to become the philosopher of the institution. Well, with Professor Fichte you agreed, or else you were in error.

(6) *The intellectual and political unity of the nation requires but a single central university for the education of its elite.* Being interested neither in higher education for the masses nor in the training of a sufficient number of professional men, Fichte recommended a single university for the education of the intellectual elite of the nation. He gave three arguments in favor of a central state university. First, science and philosophy admitted of but one unified *Geist*, by which he presumably meant the method of rational inquiry. From this single "spirit" he curiously deduced the necessity of reducing the existing provincial universities to a single institution to be established in Berlin. Why he identified the provincial institutions with a "legion of spirits" following separate, irrational, or contradictory methods of thought he did not explain. It may be that he was impatient to exterminate certain remnants of religious dogmatism which continued their academic hold here and there. One suspects, however, that he was equally impatient to introduce his own philosophy as universal enlightenment and that he desired exclusive intellectual power as much as the exclusive rule of reason. That this is no unwarranted suspicion may be inferred also from the fact that Fichte nowhere in his *Plan* showed any apprehension of intolerance, or thought it necessary to provide guarantees against violations of the freedom of teaching. It was Humboldt who saw that these were imminent whenever a single "school" dominated a university.

The second argument for a single state university was that it separated young people from their families and their native environments. Fichte deemed it a great educational disadvantage for anyone to attend schools and universities near home, especially in the case of intellectually gifted young people. Home and family attachment stood in his opinion for pettiness, dependence, and narrowness, for a sentimental, phlegmatic, conventional, and irrational kind of life which was "degrading" and stultifying to a young man's rational development (§49). Closely related to this was his third argument which stated that to maintain a number of widely scattered universities was to maintain strongholds of German Philistinism and regionalism, sentiments hostile to the growth of a common German citizenship and to the unification of the German states. A central Prussian university in Berlin—and Fichte may have hoped to make it into an all-German university—would draw its students from many parts of Germany. In addition to giving them a unified intellectual outlook, it would imbue them with the importance of creating a unified nation.

When this part of his *Plan* is related to his *Addresses to the German Nation* delivered only a year later (1808) Fichte's university appears as the coping stone of a unified system of state education. In the Addresses family and private education were once more criticized for catering to selfish individual interests. For the same reason Fichte objected to poverty and insecurity: the energies of poor children were from early years, he said, devoted to fighting for their economic survival, which inevitably turned them into selfish, petty, and brutish creatures. Their nature could be changed only if the state brought them up with the youth of other classes in common public schools. These Fichte planned as economically self-sufficient and co-operative communities with ample opportunities for training and practical work in farming and crafts. They would be "schools of unselfishness." Fichte's conviction that the human race, or at any rate the nation, could not be improved through uneven progress of its separate parts prompted him to demand coeducation as well as the abolition of class and charity schools. Finally, in order to eliminate intellectual snobbery, he required that the future "scholars," too, be brought up in the common work-schools where they would learn to know and to respect manual labor. Only after this experience would they be separated from the rest of the students to attend the university. While there are striking similarities with Plato's *Republic,* Fichte required for his state a more thoroughgoing socialism and he showed a more direct concern for the mass of the common citizens of the nation.

At the university, those ultimately selected to become the elite of the nation were to live under close supervision and under their own code of honor. They were to wear a uniform, as would the encyclopedic teachers who acted as their advisers and tutors. Those who were able would pay, and those who were needy would be supported at state expense. Fichte was anxious that none of the students should have to think about economic needs, lest they forget that they "live only to serve society." They should "never regard life's needs as a motive for any sort of activity." Upon receiving the Master's degree, which, as Fichte remarked, testified not to their mastery of the seven liberal arts or any piecemeal knowledge but only to their "art of thinking," the young scholars had first claim to the most important and responsible positions in the state. They would be the new nobility, and they would replace the hereditary aristocratic class which never ceased to provoke the puritan moralist and the national socialist in Fichte.

* * *

When, in review, one attempts to estimate the importance of Fichte's educational philosophy, he is disturbed by the man's want of fundamental clarity of thought. The reason for it seems to be deeper than the fluctuation of his belief between French republicanism and Teutonic nationalism. It lies in the fact that the true object of the will and of duty is never clearly defined, as in a primarily voluntaristic philosophy it cannot be. For it is the heroic will that *wills itself* which is here the *summum bonum.* In the aims of the new education outlined in the *Addresses to the German Nation,* the same evasiveness prevailed. "You must fashion the individual," Fichte there exclaimed, "in such a way that he simply cannot will otherwise than you wish him to will." [13] This is no more than an expression of impulse, and one apparently exempt from rational check and justification.

It has been shown that not all parts of Fichte's thought remained in that twilight; and his idea of a university in particular contains insights and truths which, though largely known since Plato, were significant to the time in which they were put forth, and they remain pertinent to the discussion of educational problems today. Yet it is unfortunately true that Fichte's best ideas —those concerning the organization of knowledge and the methods of study and teaching—were contradicted by his self-righteousness and his want of humility. Had his plan been adopted, it is probable that the application of even his best ideas would have ended in the perversion of their original truth. Whatever credit he must be given for the elucidation of the theory of general or liberal education, it is impossible to call Fichte a liberal. If he, instead of Humboldt, had become Secretary of Education at the critical moment of reform, the university would have been made the chief instrument for the Fichtean moral world order. Fichte, unlike Humboldt, would scarcely have defined this order to mean the liberation of those energies by which the moral and intellectual capacities of the individual are enlarged. Instead, he would have defined it as unanimous agreement with a single system of metaphysics and ethics, and with a definite program of political action as well. As it happened, Fichte only became a professor of philosophy at Berlin, appointed on Humboldt's suggestion, and this position did not carry the power it would have, had the University been organized according to his plan. Fichte also was elected the first Rector of the institution in 1811, and in this position he did in fact attempt to force certain academic reforms, among them the suppression of dueling and drinking. He found little support from his colleagues, however, and after less than a year he resigned the rectorship. [14]

As to the inherent contradictions in Fichte's thought, one is especially worth noting in the light of recent history. In an essay *On Machiavelli* he asserted that the national state must secure its survival by any means, and that it is not bound by common laws or treaties. It is obvious that a university which, according to Fichte, defends the principle of free rational critique and is dedicated to the search of inclusive and universal truth, cannot exist in such a state. When the Second German Empire came into being, and especially after Treitschke first honored him,[15] Fichte the nationalist began to achieve greater prominence than Fichte the rationalist. Even in the moderate judgment of Meinecke, Fichte is credited with having lent nationalism the pathos of a great ideal.[16] Whether Fichte actually would have supported the destructive and fanatically exclusive form of German nationalism under Hitler is uncertain: his stubborn Protestantism and his delight in resisting persecution speak against the assumption. In pure thought, however, his boastful nationalism as expressed in the Addresses was already so extreme and so exclusive that action could hardly have made it more complete. This is the opinion of Santayana, and I find it just.[17]

The conclusion is inevitable that Fichte's philosophy not only suffered from inherent contradictions, it also helped to promote the political abuse of the most valuable of his educational ideas. While it has been shown that humanism, too, suffered from unnecessary limitations which it imposed upon itself, the defects of Idealism were more glaring and more dangerous, and its sponsorship of liberal education in Germany added less to the strength than to the insecurity and vulnerability of the very ideal of such an education. Even before this was borne out politically, it became apparent through the conflict in which Idealism was involved with modern experimental science. It will be shown that the responsibility for this conflict, which assumed a form most injurious to a general education, did not rest wholly with one side. Yet the German Idealists helped to provoke it by their often dogmatic defense of the results obtained by deductive reasoning, by their decided partiality to the dialectical as against the scientific method, and by their unwillingness to modify their teaching in the light of empirical evidence for which they showed scant respect. To describe the polemics which ensued and to weigh their significance for the further development of German liberal education will be the task of the following chapter.

CHAPTER III

THE IDOLATRY OF SCIENCE

MODERN experimental science in Germany began to develop in the 1820's. To give a few specific dates, the Society of German Scientists and Physicians was founded in 1822, and in the opinion of Werner Siemens, the industrialist and engineer, this event initiated the age of modern science.[1] In 1824 Johannes P. Mueller began his pioneer work in physiology at the University of Bonn. In 1827 Alexander von Humboldt, the famous explorer-scientist and brother of the humanist, offered a course of lectures in Berlin which introduced for the first time a large audience of educated Germans to problems of natural history and science. But an event of even greater importance was the opening of Liebig's chemical laboratory at the University of Giessen in 1826, for this was actually the beginning of the teaching of experimental science in German universities. Justus von Liebig (1803–1873) was made professor at Giessen on the recommendation of Alexander von Humboldt, and he succeeded in persuading the Hessian government to build and support a laboratory as part of the university. While laboratories had existed before as private studies in which great scientists did their work, Liebig began to introduce university students to the methods of scientific research.

At first the growth and progress of modern science in the German universities were slow. For two decades it had to struggle against the movement of *Naturphilosophie*, whose teachers sat firmly entrenched in some of the more important institutions. Under the leadership of Schelling and, to a lesser extent, Hegel this movement regarded nature as an exclusive object of speculative thought and a topic for philosophic improvisation. It assumed that a fundamental identity existed between the realms of nature and mind, and that it was for the mind to bring nature to consciousness of herself. However, it was characteristic of these philosophers that they refused to make use of the methods of observation and experiment. The attempt to explain the forces of nature with the help of quantitative measurement and mechanical laws seemed to them not only to betray a meanly utilitarian frame of mind; it was also futile. Since they saw in nature a creative whole, informed in all its parts and manifestations by a single living spirit, they believed that to know this spirit at its very source—a knowledge to which the German Idealists frankly pretended—was the only way to solve the vast enigma. Accordingly, they looked with contempt upon the slow and laborious work of experimental scientists and heaped abuse on Sir Isaac Newton for having perpetrated a mechanistic conception of the universe. To their own serious deficiencies their minds remained closed. It escaped them that all they had done was to replace the tested methods of science by pure fantasy and arbitrary ideas to which, by employing superficial arguments by analogy, they lent at times a semblance of systematic thought. One critic said justly of Schelling that it was his ambition to produce the universe as from an empty shell. It is clear that this type of philosophy and modern science were contradictory. Eventually one or the other had to leave the field.

As the first generation of modern German scientists came forth with sharp denunciations of the *Naturphilosophie*, the movement simultaneously aided in its own destruction when its representatives attempted to apply their speculations to the solution of specific problems. Their failure was complete, as could have been expected, and the absurdity of their "explanations" ridiculed the movement in the eyes even of those who remained indifferent to the development of modern science and cared little how the issue would be decided. By way of illustration, here are some of the fantasies on nature produced by those philosophers. In Schelling's writings on medicine are found passages like the following: "The activity which, as a product, is magnetism, and in its essence is sound, corresponds to the senses of feeling and hearing. To electricity and to its intrinsic quality, light, correspond the senses of scent and sight." "In the general formation of the animal kingdom, the union of the soft and the hard presents the greatest problem of nature. The gradual receding of the bone structure toward the inner part of the body is the gradual uniting of the hearing and the feeling animal. The organ of feeling is represented by all the soft parts of the body, and the organ of hearing by all the hard parts of the body." [2] A disciple of Schelling, the Norwegian Henrik Steffens, gave a course on anthropology at the University of Berlin in the winter term of 1837–1838, in which the following notes were taken: "Each organ of the human body corresponds to a certain animal, in fact is that animal. For example, the tongue, which is freely movable, moist, and slippery, is a cuttlefish or sepia. For the bone of the tongue, the hyoid bone, is not connected with any other bone of the skeleton. The sepia also has only one bone, the familiar 'os sepia.' Consequently, this bone is not attached to any other bone. Therefore, the tongue is a sepia." [3] More easily remembered than these weird statements is a brief and classic definition attributed to the "philosophers of nature": the diamond is quartz which has achieved self-consciousness.

While it is true that not all their work was of this caliber, the plain nonsense to which they had signed their names in books and lectures was sufficient to ruin them. The whole movement might thus have been buried without tears and soon forgotten, had it not been for the lasting resentment it caused among the young pioneers of science. While these were still struggling hard for recognition, an additional obstacle was put in their way in the form of the official sanction bestowed on the already bankrupt school of *Naturphilosophie*. As late as 1841, Schelling, then a pathetic figure long past his philosophic prime, was invited by Frederick William IV of Prussia, "the Romantic on the throne," to join the Academy of Science and the University of Berlin. There Schelling lectured for three years on mythology and revelation "not as an ordinary professor," as his letter of invitation read, "but as a philosopher chosen and called by God to be the teacher of his time, whose wisdom, experience, and integrity the King himself desired near him for his own fortification." [4] Once more the educated German public looked to the philosophic chair in the University of Berlin, as it had done previously under the occupancy of the powerful Hegel, as to a general intellectual tribunal. At the same time the Prussian government turned a deaf ear to Liebig's pleas for a few university laboratories. It was even offended by his criticism of Prussian medical training, for whose serious deficiencies Liebig blamed directly the government's neglect in providing modern scientific instruction. [5]

Another more personal feeling deepened the enmity between the two sides. Many of the leading German scientists of the nineteenth century had once been students under the Idealist philosophers. At that time, as impressionable youths still undecided about their main interests and careers, they were fascinated by what then seemed exciting and bold ideas. Such, for example, was Liebig's experience, who from 1820 to 1822 came under the spell of Schelling's lectures at the University of Erlangen. But when he went to Paris to study with Gay-Lussac, the spell was broken and to the end nothing remained but this bitter reminiscence: "I, too, spent part of my years of study at a university where the greatest metaphysician of the century inspired academic youth to enthusiasm and imitation. Who could resist this contagion? I, too, have gone through that period, so rich in words and ideas and so poor as far as real knowledge and serious study were concerned. It cost me two precious years of my life. I cannot describe the shock and consternation upon awakening from this delirium. How many of the most gifted and talented youths have I not seen perish in this fraud, and how many laments over lives completely ruined did I not hear later! The wrong direction in which the philosophers led the academic youth of that time . . . —speculation without purpose or aim, inability to be of any use to society—caused demagogic activities, morbid and crazy ideas about the state, reforms, and duties. Conceit, pride, vanity, and insolence, the lame ambition which gives itself its own excessive praise because of lack of recognition from the rest of the world, were produced in the lecture halls of those men." [6]

Two facts are significant in this criticism which was representative of most scientists' feelings. One is its manner of treating the philosophers. Except for Schopenhauer's abusive comments, the German Idealists were here for the first time rudely knocked off their pedestals. Divested of all their "higher" pretensions, their deficiencies appeared to the scientist gross and glaring. They were suspected of stubborn egotism and even, as Liebig hinted, of outright imposture. But whatever the personal opinion of the scientist in this matter, his general criticism of the Idealists' mannerisms was bound to be merciless. To his sober, painstaking, and matter-of-fact type of mind, the moral pathos and pontifical pronunciamentos of the philosophers, in fact the whole aura of their lecturing, seemed out of place in a university and most incongruous with the new spirit of inquiry which was forming in the first laboratories.

The other fact of even greater significance which came to light in Liebig's criticism was a growing inclination among the scientists to condemn not only the particular school of philosophy which held up their progress, but all philosophy. This general hostility led eventually to the virtual isolation of science from philosophy within the universities, and it remained a powerful discord in German intellectual life for the rest of the century. The issue was perhaps most fairly stated by Hermann von Helmholtz (1821–1894), a scientist of more moderate judgment and broader interests than Liebig. Speaking of Hegel's philosophy and its ambition in the field of science, Helmholtz said: "It started with the hypothesis that not only spiritual phenomena, but even the actual world—nature, that is, and man—were the result of an act of thought on the part of a creative mind, similar in kind, it was supposed, to the human mind. On this hypothesis it seemed competent for the human mind, even without the guidance of external experience, to think over again the thoughts of the creator and to rediscover them by its own inner activity. Such was the view with which the 'Philosophy of Identity' set to work to construct *a priori* the results of other sciences. The process might be more or less successful in theology, law, politics, language, art, history, in short in all sciences the subject matter of which really grows out of our moral nature, and which are therefore properly classed together under the name of moral sciences. . . . But even granting that Hegel was more or less successful in constructing, *a priori*, the leading results of the moral sciences, still it was no proof of the correctness of the hypothesis of Identity with which he started. The facts of nature would have been the crucial test. . . . If nature really reflected the result of the thought of a creative mind, the system ought, without difficulty, to find a place for her comparatively simple phenomena and processes. It was at this point that Hegel's philosophy, we venture to say, utterly broke down. His system of nature seemed, at least to natural philosophers, absolutely crazy. Of all the distinguished scientific men who were his contemporaries, not one was found to stand up for his ideas. Accordingly, Hegel himself, convinced of the importance of winning for his philosophy in the field of physical science that recognition which had been so freely accorded to it elsewhere, launched out with unusual vehemence and acrimony against the natural philosophers and especially against Sir Isaac Newton. . . . The philosophers accused the scientific men of narrowness; the scientific men retorted that the philosophers were crazy. And so it came about that men of science began to lay some stress on the banishment of all philosophic influences from their work; while some of them, including men of the greatest acuteness, went so far as to condemn philosophy altogether, not merely as useless, but as mischievous dreaming." [7]

Since Idealism in its various forms was all the philosophy German scientists had known, the rift was indeed inevitable. Yet it was unfortunate. Scientists might honestly think that philosophy was useless and irrelevant to their work, an idea which continued concentration on the foreground of fact and experiment gradually turned into a fixed belief. But actually science rested on certain assumptions and employed conceptions which it never proved, and these constituted nothing less than a metaphysics. The fact that many men of science remained unconscious of its hidden presence merely meant that they were apt to be uncritical of their favorite hypotheses and that they remained unaware of the limitations of science as a whole. Complete rebellion against philosophy, therefore, would in all probability end by stunting the growth of their own minds and impairing their susceptibility to ideas of non-scientific origin. Furthermore, reasoning exclusively in terms of condition and cause, force and necessity, would easily lead any mind to assume that all of reality could be reduced to a mechanism and described in chemical and physical terms. This was in fact the prejudice shared by the majority of scientists of that period. "Throughout the nineteenth century," says Dampier, "most men of science, consciously or unconsciously, held the common-sense view that matter, its primary properties, and their relations, as revealed by science, are ultimate realities, and that human bodies are mechanisms perhaps occasionally controlled or influenced by minds. When they thought about ultimate scientific concepts, many physicists realized that these opinions, convenient as working assumptions, would not stand critical examination; but, in the laboratory as in practical life, there was no time for philosophic doubt." [8]

The limitations of this uncritical materialism were revealed at the end of the century by revolutionary developments in science itself, and they were eventually exposed also by philosophers. Here scientific materialism is examined chiefly for its educational implications, and particularly for its influence upon the projection of new aims of university study. For it soon became apparent that the whole dispute, once it had achieved its more immediate goal of securing for modern science an important place in the university, culminated in the attempt of the scientists to replace the Idealists' conception of the university with one of their own. Thus the quarrel shifted to a new plane on which the older arguments recurred but took on a more general educational significance. The problem to be decided was, which of the two factions should determine the methods and aims of university teaching. Obviously there was little promise of a fair decision on either part. The scientists opposed the philosophers because they, prejudiced against nature and ignorant of her laws, had dictated to science. On the other hand, the scientists, provoked into often reckless opposition, denied or were embarrassed by the existence of human values and purposes which could not be fitted into a mechanical order of things. Under these conditions it was improbable that the scientists, even when speaking for the university as a whole, would show an understanding of the humanities or even admit the possibility of approaching the study of their own subject with a humanistic interest. The latter part of this chapter will describe in greater detail the difficulties in which scientists found themselves when they attempted to assume the role of educators and educational philosophers.

Meanwhile the great quarrel progressed beyond the stage of acrimonious dispute over general views and began to have practical consequences. University scientists, pressing forward, sought to obtain the necessary buildings and equipment for the expansion of scientific instruction. Liebig campaigned vigorously. But laboratories in Prussian universities were not established until after 1860, although in the universities of some of the smaller states a few were found before that time, notably at Marburg under Bunsen, at Göttingen under Wöhler, and at Giessen under Liebig. During the time needed to convince the state governments of the importance of modern science, its teachers found another issue worth fighting for. It was a curious fact that with all the bitter words flung back and forth between them, the representatives of science and the humanities remained united in one department, in the faculty of philosophy.[9] At its meetings physicists and philologists, chemists and historians, physiologists and philosophers continued to sit side by side. At last the scientists arose to complain that they were outnumbered and that the opposing majority abused its power by vetoing the necessary funds for scientific instruments and teaching equipment. They further argued that since science would soon grow into many sciences, the faculty of philosophy would grow too large to be effectively administered as one. They therefore suggested that it be divided into two independent departments. The issue was discussed after the middle of the century in most German universities. Only in one, however, the University of Tübingen in 1863, was a separate department of science established.[10] There the decision was reached largely through the agitation of the physiologist Hugo von Mohl, with the professors of medicine on his side. Mohl, conscious that he was breaking an ancient tradition, justified the division in his opening address to the new department with the following reasons: "The establishment of the faculty of natural sciences means a break with the medieval view that culture can be found only in humanistic studies. It means the recognition of the fact that the natural sciences have grown to equality with the other branches of learning, that they must pursue their special purpose in their own way, and the assurance that they may strive toward the accomplishment of this purpose without being led astray by foreign influences."[11]

In spite of Mohl's efforts to make the division of the faculty of philosophy an issue of major importance, it did not become such for two reasons. One was practical. When laboratories and chairs for science finally were established—and this happened on a large scale after the Franco-Prussian War had persuaded governments of the military and industrial value of science—the future of scientific instruction and research in the universities was assured regardless of the opinions of envious and hostile professors in other fields. The other was an ideal reason. Though Mohl gave the appearance of speaking in the interest of all scientists, he actually expressed only the opinion of a more extreme group. This was opposed by another, more moderate group which in the end proved the more influential one. It included such well-known men of science as Helmholtz, the brothers Paul and Emil Du Bois-Reymond, A. W. Hofmann and Lothar Meyer. These men rejected the proposed division because they saw in it the beginning of isolation between the different branches of knowledge, a development which to them threatened to dissolve the university into narrowly specialized professional and technical schools. Here, rather unexpectedly, new defenders arose for an older conception of university study. Despite the hostile feelings and inner frictions which existed, to a moderate group of scientists, at least, the university remained the ideal form in which the totality of systematic knowledge should be organized.

As welcome as such a thread of continuity is to the historian, its importance must not be exaggerated. Traditions are frequently affirmed by people who no longer understand their basic values but borrow their hallowed name. Thus, though nineteenth-century scientists did attempt to preserve the *universitas litterarum*, their reasons were novel and different from those of the Idealists and humanists a few decades before. Some scientists, whose most intelligent spokesman was Helmholtz, hoped that all branches of learning would fall under the influence of modern science, in which case the universities promised to become the largest and most productive research centers that a scientist's heart could desire. They also believed that it would be to the advantage of all other branches of knowledge if the standards, methods, and mode of thought of modern science were extended to them.

Here and there, however, an individual scientist could be found whose affirmation of the traditional German conception of the university was not prompted by partisanship alone. How many there were it is impossible to say, but they certainly were the exception to the rule. In fact only one, the chemist Lothar Meyer, is known to have reminded his colleagues that universities were institutions charged with the responsibility of *general* education. In his opinion, this responsibility was all the graver in a civilization becoming increasingly technical. With an awareness of cultural problems and a foresight extremely rare among his colleagues, Meyer warned that the influence of liberal and humanizing education upon the national culture was already being diminished by the rapid rise of technical schools whose purpose was to train the growing mass of engineers, mechanics, technical experts, and assistants of all sorts. These technical schools were completely separate from the universities and the secondary schools in administration, history, and purpose. To Meyer this separation portended the eventual emancipation of technical training from liberal education in Germany, and he foresaw the fatal consequences which such a development must bring. That he should have foreseen them so much more clearly than any university man of science may well be explained by the fact that he was himself a teacher in one of the newer technological institutes and in a position to observe at first hand the trend of their development. To understand Meyer's anxiety and the gravity of the problems he discussed, a brief sketch of the history of technical education in Germany is here in order.

In the eighteenth century Germany possessed only a small number of *Realschulen*, among which Hecker's in Berlin (1747) may be specially mentioned. Early in the nineteenth century most German states and larger cities began to establish trade and technical schools of an elementary type. Students entered as young as twelve with no other preparation than arithmetic and writing. Teachers were frequently graduates from these same schools and therefore lacked breadth of knowledge. Since these early technical schools devoted themselves to specialized vocational training, their instruction precluded any theoretical foundation or systematic knowledge. As a rule they were placed, in contrast to the secondary schools and universities, under the administrative control of departments of commerce or city boards of trade, as if to indicate that immediate utility and not education was expected of them. Between 1830 and 1860 many of the elementary technical schools expanded into poly-

technical institutions, and of these some were reorganized after
1860 as higher institutes of technology which toward the end
of the century received the name *Technische Hochschulen*.
The leader in this development was the Technological Institute of Karlsruhe, which achieved university rank in 1865 and
in which Meyer taught. It then required for entrance, like the
universities, completion of the secondary school and, by including in its curriculum mathematics and the theory of science,
it could justly claim to have become a school of higher systematic
studies.

While this was a long way from the narrow vocational interests which the technical schools had served only a few decades
before, they still could not be compared to the universities by
a student seeking a balanced education. This was Meyer's main
argument.[12] Perhaps because he did not belong to a university,
its great tradition and its educational opportunities appeared
to him more admirable than an inside critic might have admitted. Meyer once more referred to the earlier intolerance of
philosophy toward empirical science and its contempt for the
utilitarian affairs of life, to which he ascribed the divorce of
technical training from university education. But as an ardent
supporter of the university, he maintained that since the middle
of the century conditions had been created which made a
union of universities and technical institutes both possible and
desirable. No great adjustment would be required of either, since
—he wrote in 1873—the universities had largely replaced deductive reasoning and metaphysical interest by empirical methods
in nearly all branches of learning. On this new and uniform
foundation—and here he agreed with Helmholtz—the unity
of *Wissenschaft* could be renewed. However, he believed that
the technological institutes would profit most from the proposed
union. They would share in the greater intellectual freedom and
more systematic thinking which prevailed in the universities.
There only, he thought, was found disinterested scientific
inquiry. There a more productive type of work was stimulated
by the close relationship and interaction between all the sciences.

Last but not least, in the universities the study of science was supplemented by the equally important study of culture. Should the union fail, Meyer warned, inestimable damage might be done. The steadily growing number of people required to run the machinery of modern civilization would be deprived of a liberal education. Experts, specialists, and managers would occupy positions of social power and control but, being absorbed in the problems of efficient production and organization, they would lack any appreciation of human values.

It may be doubted whether Meyer's suggestion was really practical. The great size of the institution which would have resulted from the proposed union would certainly have produced disadvantages and new problems. Universities and *Technische Hochschulen* remained, in fact, separate. But Meyer had recognized the crucial problem of education in modern technical civilization—how to prevent the separation of technical power from moral responsibility. Another solution was tried near the end of the century by introducing into the *Technische Hochschulen* courses dealing with the history, present status, and problems of culture and society. However, the increasing demands made by highly specialized training left technology students little or no time to attend these classes. New efforts to provide at least the opportunity and to urge the importance of liberal education for these students were made under the Weimar Republic, especially in the *Technische Hochschule Dresden* on the initiative of the Saxon Ministry of Education.[13] After 1933 the whole problem, together with so many others, was drowned in the wave of political ballyhoo and fanaticism. For the Nazis, who desired only animated automata in place of responsible citizens, the problem had ceased to exist.

To return, however, to the group of scientists who wished to preserve the university because they hoped to make it the vehicle of their own interests. Even these men, it must be admitted, caught a glimpse of the probable dangers which would attend the admission of a separatist, or departmental, spirit into higher learning. Helmholtz in 1862, Emil Du Bois-

Reymond in 1877, and A. W. Hofmann in 1880, delivered academic addresses[14] in which they reaffirmed the belief that the university was the only institution capable of balancing the student's intellectual interests. They even warned that unvaried research work with its required specialized training impoverishes the imagination because it deprives the mind of opportunities for comprehensive thought. They added that research and instruction in science themselves would suffer if science were to be divorced from humanistic studies. Yet, upon closer examination, one realizes that these men never really came to grips, with the problems they hinted at. And as they proceeded to suggest their own solutions, they only revealed how deeply their special interests had already biased their general thinking on education.

The first evidence of this bias may be seen in the assumption that the purposes of a university and of natural science are identical. If at the time this was not yet wholly true, the representative opinion among scientists was that it soon would be. Pointing to the growing application of empirical methods to many branches of knowledge and human activity, Helmholtz said: "I do think that our age has learned many lessons from the physical sciences. The absolute, unconditional reverence for facts, and the fidelity with which they are collected, a certain distrustfulness of appearances, the effort to detect in all cases relations of cause and effect, and the tendency to assume their existence, which distinguish our century from preceding ones, seem to me to point to such an influence."[15]

On the assumption that all departments of the university would uniformly adopt the methods and mode of thought characteristic of physical science, it was natural to expect from the institution a more closely co-ordinated and more productive research. German scientists of the mid-nineteenth century frequently stressed the fact that progress in one field depended upon progress in others. This was true especially in sciences only just emerging. Physiology, for example, then a new field, was said by Johannes Mueller and Liebig to be in need of such assistance as more developed sciences could give it. There were numerous other illustrations. Liebig demonstrated the bearing of chemistry on agriculture, and Wöhler's synthesis of urea broke down the older distinction between organic and inorganic matter. Helmholtz' research on the physiological basis of musical sensations was another case in point. All this proved that scientists had real reasons for wanting to preserve the *universitas litterarum;* the advantages *they* derived from it were undeniable. Only they forgot to ask whether their meat might not be other men's poison. They were unconcerned as to whether the uniform application of methods useful and adequate to them might not disastrously narrow the scope and deflect from the true aim of such pursuits as philosophy, history, and, in fact, education. Helmholtz, for example, denied to philosophy any claims beyond "the criticism of the sources of cognition and the definition of the functions of the intellect." This was to bar philosophy from all inquiry into the deeper questions of the nature of reality and the meaning of life. Here was a second demonstration of the scientist's preoccupation with his own interests.

In the third instance, there was the belief that progress in knowledge, which Helmholtz thought to be the chief purpose of the university, was achieved most visibly and certainly through the advancement of science. Helmholtz spoke almost movingly of the new spirit which had recently come into the university from its research laboratories. Since their appearance, he said, controversy and argumentation survived only as the relics of a past age when men, their positions fixed by *a priori* thought, had been contemptuous of observation and experiment because they would not learn from one another, or from fresh experience. He seemed to imply that this characterization was true of all branches of non-scientific knowledge and, of course, especially of philosophy. He went on to contrast the older individualistic and dogmatic type of intellectual with the modern experimental scientist who knew better than to want singly to solve the riddle of the universe. This type was bringing with him a new code of ethics in which patience, modesty, co-operation, and unselfishness were the cardinal virtues. "Let each of us think of himself," Helmholtz wrote, "not as a man seeking to satisfy his own thirst for knowledge, to promote his own private advantage, or to shine by his own abilities, but rather as a fellow laborer in one great common work." [16]

This whole conception of a university, besides its general bias and occasional misrepresentations, troubles one by its virtual evasion of all problems of education. One is persuaded to believe that education, somehow and somewhere, *accrues* while knowledge is being gathered. Education, so to speak, *happens* to a student; it is, as the thoughtless jargon of our day has it, a "process." To participate in the collective enterprise of laboratory research, according to Helmholtz, is to submit to a kind of moral and mental discipline. That such discipline may be valuable is granted. But the fact is that only advanced students may participate in the research Helmholtz was speaking of. He himself, reported to have disliked teaching and to have been a poor lecturer on elementary physics,[17] was interested only in working with small groups of gifted graduate students. This perhaps explains best why, even though he was discussing the general problems of university education, he failed to concern himself with the peculiar difficulties of teaching the great mass of elementary students.

Nor was this all. Scientists themselves admitted that absorption in highly specialized research, to the exclusion of other interests, was detrimental to a young man's general grasp of the field. Helmholtz himself became alarmed at the fact that, with the increase of scientific knowledge, the interest and work of the individual scientist progressively narrowed. In his address on *The Aim and Progress of Physical Science* (1869), delivered less than a decade after he had set forth his idea of a university, he urged his colleagues to meet regularly so that they might review together the latest results of scientific progress. The division of labor in the sciences, he said, was growing at such a rate that it threatened to put them out of touch with each other. He thought it necessary, therefore, that they make an effort to relate their special contributions to the whole. It was the only way by which, in his opinion, the individual scientist could perceive the meaning of his work and from this obtain the satisfaction he needed to carry on. A very similar, even more eloquent warning came from the physiologist Du Bois-Reymond.[18] The progress of science, he said with resignation, was not all glory; there was a cost to pay. He looked back with nostalgia to such a work as Alexander von Humboldt's *Cosmos*, a treatise which, in addition to its scientific qualities, possessed philosophic breadth and historical perspective, literary distinction and an esthetic feeling for nature. These broad sympathies, Du Bois-Reymond feared, had in the second part of the century been sacrificed under the pressure of specialized experimental work. The lauded progress of science, to which society was beginning to owe so much, demanded from its students a type of work which threatened to impoverish their own lives.

If these reports truly describe the conditions—and what could be more trustworthy than the testimony of the men of science themselves?—no severer criticism of research as education was possible. But it escaped these same scientists that to admit the educational defectiveness of research was inconsistent with their idea of a university. Obviously Helmholtz was forced into this contradiction by the fundamental bias of his thought: for having narrowed the purpose of the university to the advancement of science, he was driven to cull from science more than it could possibly yield. Research, he frankly admitted, was no longer self-rewarding and self-justifying. It had become an occupation which made reflection difficult and was likely to thwart other interests a man might have. The value of the individual Helmholtz assessed in terms of the value of his contribution to science. He put him into a form of servitude and offered him as compensation the pride of sharing in the progress of knowledge. "Each student," he said, "must be content to find his reward in rejoicing over new discoveries. . . . He must rest satisfied with the consciousness that he, too, has contributed something to the increasing fund of knowledge on which the dominion of man over all forces hostile to intelligence rests." [19]

With these words, spoken with such gentle resignation that one nearly overlooks their ominousness, the scientist dispatched liberal education to its grave. To the earlier Idealists and humanists, education had meant the achievement of individual judgment, breadth of knowledge, balance of interests, and that awareness of self in relation to others which is the condition of responsible action. These universal values have, in varying forms and with different emphases, been the substance of all liberal theories of education since Plato and Aristotle. They were reaffirmed, as the earlier parts of this study have shown, in the humanism of Wilhelm von Humboldt; and in German Idealism too—vitiated though it was by its inherent dogmatism—the self had striven, from an old feeling of Protestant responsibility, to give account of itself and its relations to the world. Now this tradition came to an end in the scientists' conception of the university. Helmholtz, for one, merely asked devotion to a vaguely conceived "cause," usually described as progress. Its devotees were asked to throw their souls into the bargain and then hope for the best. This was a frank renunciation of the individual's quest for a rational and responsible order embracing his *whole* life. The conflict between nineteenth-century science and liberal education could not have been more clearly and more radically stated.

This unfortunate development, by which many university men came to conceive of science as the enemy of the humanities, was by no means inevitable. It would also be an error to impute to all teachers of science the opinions expressed by Helmholtz. For example, at the annual meeting of the Society of German Scientists and Physicians in 1889, a professor of medicine proposed that the Society urge all German universities to establish chairs for the history of science.[20] A knowledge of this subject should be required of all students of science and medicine in order to counteract the growing utilitarian interest among them, which the speaker believed to be the most conspicuous result of the narrow specialization of university studies. Here was a recommendation which, if acted upon, could have resolved the conflict between science and the humanities. For it could have been shown that in contrast to the purely professional or research interest in science, the history of scientific thought offered excellent possibilities for humanist teaching. Here the broader relations of science to religion, cosmology, and philosophy could have been discussed. Students could have been given a sense of the evolution and gradual refinement of what finally becomes known in science as an objective truth. They could have been taught to understand that scientific ideas have their source in human imagination and judgment, and that it is on these that the advancement of science depends. If teachers of science had placed their emphasis upon these aspects, then they would no longer have been in conflict with liberal teaching. For whatever the subject, liberal teaching aims to help students develop the powers by which they may understand, maintain, and add to the achievements in arts and sciences. Unfortunately, however, it was not these but Helmholtz' ideas of the teaching of science and of university study which remained representative in the nineteenth and even into the twentieth century.

Once Helmholtz was forced to admit that research was a grossly deficient method of education, he shifted his defense to other grounds. Scientific research, he said, was beginning to yield tremendous benefits to society. It made possible industrial progress and greater material welfare for the mass of people. Could it not be argued and urged, therefore, as a moral duty? If the individual researcher realized that eventually his work would be of use to others, even though he had no control over its application, could one not say that he was receiving an education in the service of society? "To extend the limits of science," Helmholtz wrote, "is really to work for the progress of humanity." Here he was getting himself into even deeper difficulties. His thinking ended in a muddle characteristic of some of our present-day discussions of "social education": a vague, wishful humanitarianism was brought in to cover up the superficiality and the fallacy of his educational ideas.

It is further significant that even such a disinterested scientist as Helmholtz fell under the influence of that nineteenth-century optimism which was perhaps most eloquently and most fatuously expressed by Macaulay in his famous controversy with Robert Southey. To make propaganda for a popular science can originally have been scarcely congenial to such university men as Helmholtz. Yet they fell in with the popularizers when they mistook progress in science for universal progress, or when they assumed that an ampler supply and a greater perfection of technical means would automatically bring about the realization of human ends. Like so many others, Helmholtz seemed not to regard human ideals and values as individual achievements and, in consequence, of no importance in education. He rather inclined to regard them as natural endowments, or things to be taken for granted. This misconception explains why, when speaking on behalf of the work of the university as a whole, he could think only of the advancement of knowledge and gave no thought whatever to the problem of so integrating and realizing knowledge in individual human beings that it might contribute to their achieving moral and intellectual maturity. It is true that he spoke of the "moral purposes" of man subjecting the forces of nature. He may have been able to answer for himself what these purposes were. But to take them for granted in young students was unjustified and educationally irresponsible. For by leaving the moral life uncultivated and its purposes undefined, he invited that heedless preoccupation with technology which has helped to precipitate the catastrophe of German culture. One need only remind himself of the growth of German nationalism which paralleled that of modern German science, to realize the ominousness of the situation. As the sense of individual responsibility diminished and withered away, nationalism—that "heroic infirmity," as a great German of the eighteenth century had called it—was ready to fill the void. It is not denied that there were occasionally teachers in German universities who urged the clarification of individual purpose and criticism of social action, who cultivated appreciation of human values, and who encouraged rational thinking among their students. Yet the general impression is that universities were research centers and that teaching was incidental.[21] The majority of professors in science and, as the following chapter will show, in the humanities as well, were absorbed in the task of accumulating knowledge. This productivity, the results of which were visible enough, was what impressed the outside world, and especially in the United States colleges and universities began to rival it. The human void which yawned under that bustling productivity and the moral default which were its price escaped those naïve admirers. Even today, the collapse of the German universities and the submission of their staffs to National Socialism in 1933 seem to those admirers in no way related to the disintegration which had begun to take place much earlier.

So much for the scientists' conception of the university. To conclude this chapter, certain views held by leading German scientists concerning the relation of science to culture must be briefly discussed. That these views, expressed near the end of the century, should still derive from, or at least be deeply colored by, the earlier quarrel with the philosophers is to be expected. It is, however, a surprise to find that they also reveal the failure of what scientists had been most determined to achieve: the elimination of philosophy, if not from the entire university, at least from their own province. It was there precisely that its ghost returned to haunt them. It came as a reminder that philosophy in the form of rational and conscientious inquiry into the meaning of human existence could not be suppressed unless it was at the expense of consistent and imaginative thought itself. Moreover, the scientists had not reckoned with the national intellectual climate. Deny it as they might, they inherited the propensity for system building at a time when the Idealist systems themselves had nearly lost their power.[22] Yet the sad fact was that for men who were intolerant of all interests except their own, there remained little with which to build. Thus vapid and wholly unwarranted generalizations of certain scientific hypotheses came to take the place of serious philosophy.

Already in mid-century there had been some who preached noisily the gospel of the omnipotence of science. The most successful were the leaders of German Scientific Materialism, Büchner (1824–1899), Vogt (1817–1895), and Moleschott (1822–1893). Philosophically speaking, these men did little more than to revive the ideas of eighteenth-century French materialism, which they revised in the light of more recent scientific work. The novelty of the movement they led was in the effective popularization of those ideas. They succeeded in promoting among certain sections of the people—notably among intelligent workingmen—a lasting hostility toward orthodox Christianity. In time this allied itself with Marxism. This scientific "enlightenment," carried on by the Materialists in numerous public lectures and literary works of many editions,[23] was characterized throughout by a crude simplification of major problems. Ultimate reality, for example, was found in dead matter; consciousness was reduced to lower forms of existence; the various functions of organisms, psychological and biological, were explained as nothing but chemical or mechanical reactions. To give but one crass illustration, the brain, according to Moleschott, secretes thought as the kidneys secrete urine or the liver bile. As a result of their radical views, the three Materialists were compelled to resign from their positions in German universities where they had been teachers of science.

Orthodox churchmen were not the only ones to attack them. A scientist of the rank of Rudolf Virchow also denounced the movement because he feared that unless serious men of science clearly dissociated themselves from it, their work too was likely to suffer from the religious reaction which had been aroused. He stated publicly, therefore, that modern science did not necessarily promote a materialistic view of life, and he doubted that science was as yet in a position to develop a philosophy of its own. However, he shared with other moderates such as Helmholtz the belief that scientific methods could be successfully applied to social problems in which man's failure remained most conspicuous.[24]

A more unqualified belief in scientific and universal progress is met again in Emil Du Bois-Reymond. In a public lecture entitled "Kulturgeschichte und Kulturwissenschaft" (1877) this scientist attempted to assess the comparative values of cultural history and the history of science. Whatever impression of being a critical or even pessimistic thinker Du Bois-Reymond had given in his famous *Ignorabimus* speech, his opinions expressed here were of opposite quality. He proclaimed that there had never been a greater period in the history of civilization than the nineteenth century, when for the first time science furnished culture with a stable and lasting foundation. Classical Greece, he admitted, had made great intellectual and artistic contributions; but, because its foundations were not technologically sound, it lasted only a short while. Modern man, on the contrary, had confidence in the means put into his hands by science. They gave him a consciousness of his own power so that he could dispense with the ideals of bygone ages. Under the influence of science modern man's conception of history itself was transformed. It was no longer that inconclusive process of change, of wars, revolutions, and uncontrolled force which traditional historians had made it out to be. There was no sense, he said, in contemplating the murky streams of human passion. That could only result in pessimism about the future. Instead history should be rewritten from the scientist's point of view: for he would record only the victories over slavery and superstition, pain and disease, and thus demonstrate the universal progress of mankind. As for the disquieting problems of his own age, such as the growth of German nationalism, the threats of future wars and social revolution, Du Bois-Reymond felt that there was no need to be alarmed. If those human problems became oppressive, there was always, he said, the vastness of the universe in which the scientist could take refuge: within its dimensions those problems appeared insignificant. Besides there was always one's own special work to attend to.

It is clear, and the critical discussions in the next chapter will make it clearer still, that such ideas were symptoms of a failure of nerve and general cultural decay. A similar bias against history and scorn of the humanities, the same forced optimism and evasion of moral and social problems were evident also in two other eminent men of science, Ernst Haeckel (1834-1919) and Wilhelm Ostwald (1853-1932). Of the two Haeckel was perhaps the more influential. As a professor of zoology at the University of Jena he had done remarkable research and field work on deep-sea organisms. But he is better known as the most ardent follower and exponent of Darwin in Germany. Under his leadership the theory of evolution hardened into a universal dogma which Darwin himself would hardly have accepted. "The acceptance of the theory of evolution produced the illusion that an insight into the method by which the result had been obtained had given a complete solution of the problem, and that a knowledge of man's origin and history had laid bare the nature of his inward spirit as well as the structure of the human organism as regarded from without." [25]

Haeckel's "philosophy" found its most comprehensive expression in The Riddle of the Universe (1899), a book which had an astonishing popular success.[26] Though he asserted that his was not a materialistic philosophy—he called it Monism—Haeckel's views were bluntly reductionist. He maintained, for example, that chemical properties of carbon were the sole cause of life, which originated by spontaneous generation from inorganic matter. Psychic activity he explained by reducing it to chemical changes, in which form it was to be found in every living cell, a belief which caused Haeckel to speak of "cell souls." The so-called higher faculties of the human mind were only the sum total of the psychic functions of the cells of the brain. Man had developed like other mammals from lower forms of life, from which he differed only in degree and not in kind. The idea of the freedom of the human will, for example, was but a leftover from the ancient superstition about the divine origin of man. Nature was thoroughly determined by the laws of the conservation of matter and energy, which made immortality and a non-natural God impossible. The only meaningful interpretation of immortality was the preservation of matter throughout all chemical changes, and of God, that he was the sum total of atomic forces and "ether vibrations."

In addition to this cosmology, Haeckel offered a monistic ethics. It imposed two equally important duties on man, one to himself and the other to society, but both were only different forms of the fundamental will to survive. Haeckel scorned Christian ethics for its depreciation of sex, for its suppression of healthy egotism and for exaggerating the virtue of loving one's neighbor. On metaphysical questions Haeckel declared a general ban, for to admit their existence would have meant that the solution of the riddles of the universe, as he attempted it, was impossible. It irritated him to have people ask questions for which there existed no scientific method of solution. "Let us leave the fruitless brooding over ideal phantoms to the 'pure metaphysicians,' " he cried, "and let us instead as 'real physicists' rejoice in the immense progress which has actually been made by our monistic philosophy of nature." [27] As precursors of his Monism he claimed Spinoza, Goethe, and Kant. Such presumption and ignorance of philosophy Friedrich Paulsen criticized sharply and with justifiable indignation. [28]

Wilhelm Ostwald, professor of chemistry at the University of Leipzig and Nobel prize winner in 1909, was a "philosophic" disciple of Haeckel. His brand of Monism, preached more frankly as a religion than Haeckel's, was based on the principle of energy rather than on the theory of evolution. In asserting that energy, not dead matter, was the ultimate reality, Ostwald too believed that he had outgrown the earlier scientific materialism. From the basic law of the preservation of energy he derived an ethics, the categorical imperative of which was summed up in the simple formula, "Don't waste energy!" This was his solution of the problem of values, and it served him as the theme for many Monistic Sunday sermons which he delivered as president of the Association of German Monists, founded in 1904.[29] These sermons were meant as a sort of pep talk to ordinary people on the ordinary problems of life. But Ostwald also concerned himself there with the relation of the individual to society and with the aims of education. The individual, Ostwald preached, must transform his given share of raw energy into the specific energy of the occupation most useful to society, taking care never to waste an ounce of it. For man's worth was measured in units of specific energy delivered to society. Education was of value only in so far as it increased the efficiency of this turnover. It was, in other words, simply a branch of technology. The German universities, Ostwald complained, continued to indulge, even in this scientific age, in the most glaringly inefficient activities. Most backward in this respect seemed to him the humanities, to which he referred as *Papierwissenschaften*. They were wholly incapable of predicting future developments and did nothing to encourage man with optimistic prospects as did science and technology. In fact, they were a drag on progress, for they assumed the didactic attitude of old men and sent youth back to the past for human wisdom and ideals. Life would be happier, he said, without these retrospective cults, and if by chance the moldy treasures of humanistic learning were destroyed, mankind would suffer no loss.

It is unnecessary to go into a detailed criticism of these scientific philosophers. Their sophistry and glibness in passing over all the deeper problems are obvious enough. Yet it is curious to see how, after having demolished the stately systems of Idealist philosophy, they built their own temples of devotion. Having denied responsibility and freedom to human life, they invested the atom with a singular dignity and restored the soul to the cell. Their complete disrespect for tradition, their incapacity to distinguish between the world of fact and the world of value, and their reduction of the human person to a thoroughly determined mechanism constitute an emphatic denial that education is a moral problem at all. For them it has, in fact, become a branch of technology. It is as a protest against this dehumanization that the educational criticism of Nietzsche and others, presented in the following chapter, assumes its real significance.

CHAPTER IV

CRITICISM AND SATIRE OF ACADEMIC CULTURE: NIETZSCHE

THE sincere philosopher, Nietzsche said in *Beyond Good and Evil*, has always been the bad conscience of society. He himself was the bad conscience of nineteenth-century Germany and to some extent of Europe also. Like an irritating *scrupulus* he tried to work himself into the boots of the striding and strutting new Reich. In his earlier works, which are essays in cultural criticism, his purpose was to warn the nation against its pride, its boastfulness, and its material preoccupations. In the role of the unwanted critic Nietzsche was of course not alone. Numerous others, such as Carlyle, Kierkegaard, Burckhardt, Ibsen, D. H. Lawrence, Marx, and Tolstoy shared in the task of exposing what they believed were the vices of nineteenth-century civilization, much though they differed and contradicted each other's ideals and remedies. Of them all Nietzsche was most seriously concerned with education. More precisely, he devoted himself to exposing the faults and the shams of German higher education, and to fighting what he himself realized was the losing battle of humanism.

The works of Nietzsche most relevant to this study are the *Unzeitgemässen Gedanken*, in four parts (1873–1876), usually translated as *Thoughts Out of Season; The Birth of Tragedy* (1871); and a series of five lectures entitled *The Future of Our Educational Institutions* (1872). All of these belong to his youthful period when he was still a professor at the University of Basle. There will be occasional references to his later, more philosophical works. Primarily, however, this chapter is devoted to Nietzsche the critic, not to Nietzsche the philosopher, though of course the two are organically related. Intense dissatisfaction with modern civilization and what it had done to man was the source of Nietzsche's utopian society to be ruled by a new type of man. His solitary vision inspired a number of Germans, among them the disciples of the poet George, who will be dealt with in the following chapter. With respect to his cultural criticism, however, the essays mentioned are the most relevant and informative. They were written from a personal knowledge of nineteenth-century academic conditions and contain many acute analyses and observations. The vision of the superman was as yet in its first dawn, and the tendency to speculation and aphorism well restrained. It was the period of Nietzsche's thought during which an esthetic form of humanism remained to a large extent the basis of his criticism of culture .

Nietzsche was brought up in the classical tradition at Pforta, Bonn, and Leipzig, and in 1869, at the age of twenty-four, he became a professor of classical philology at the University of Basle. His duties included the teaching of Greek in the upper class of the *Pädagogium*, a secondary school attached to the University, so that his experience extended over several levels of the educational system. He was, from what accounts we have, a good teacher, and he might have had a brilliant academic career. But there were early premonitions that his life would be neither smooth nor serene. While still a student in Leipzig, he was oppressed by the myopia of the scholarly profession and remarked about "that teeming breed of philologists, their mole-like activities, their full pouches and blind eyes, their pleasure in the worm they catch." [1] As a young professor, he was without the ordinary ambitions for professional advancement. At least, the books he began to publish did not contribute to research but were concerned with problems quite outside his field. *The Birth of Tragedy*, for example, his first publication, was an exciting but poorly organized and hardly thought-out book in which Nietzsche stormed through philosophy and art, Greek drama, and Wagnerian opera all in one. It is not surprising that he was promptly denounced as unsound by orthodox German scholarship.[2]

This first rebuke strengthened Nietzsche's suspicion of the conventional scholar's limitations. It helped him to see more clearly that his energies were not to be mortgaged to his professional academic duties, and that his intellectual interests were other than those prescribed by orthodox scholarship and teaching. He felt that he was a free spirit, unbound by plodding labor and its banausic satisfactions. His aristocratic affinities showed early. He was a lover of form, had an eye for the natural rank and value of things, and was sensitive to human nobility and the subtlety of the human psyche. He possessed a sharp wit, malice, and a lightness of touch unusual among German writers. Obviously he was better equipped to be a critic than a professor.

Nietzsche opened his attack on German education with his lectures on *The Future of Our Educational Institutions*, which form a sort of prologue to *Thoughts Out of Season*. Surveying the field, he found two dominant trends: an increase in educational opportunity, and, accompanying it, a lowering of educational standards. A growing population and increasing wealth caused the German states to expand their systems of secondary schools and even to establish new universities—the University of Strassburg, for example, was opened immediately upon the conclusion of the Franco-Prussian War. The rapid advance of German industrialization was creating a new middle class which, he noted, came to regard the institutions of higher education as a means to the attainment of social and economic advantage. The government, eager to promote the interests of this new class and to obtain from it the larger number of administrators and officers demanded by the growing bureaucratization of life, was willing to support new schools, new universities and scientific laboratories. The Reich, by a decree of 1871, even offered a special incentive for attendance: every male student who completed at least a six-year course in a secondary school was required to give only one year, instead of the customary three, to military service. The government, he complained, further increased the bureaucratic control of education by a system of state examinations, degrees, and licenses, and spurred individual ambition by titles, honors, and promotions.

Nietzsche cited these facts as evidence for his argument that the expansion of the educational system was not caused by the growth of spontaneous intellectual interests, which for him was the only source of cultural progress, but by the increasing perversion of education to political and economic uses. This perversion drew his sharpest protest, just as it had earlier provoked Friedrich August Wolf and Wilhelm von Humboldt and all those who had fought against the dehumanization of education. Theirs was the tradition, grown feeble since, to which Nietzsche still felt loyal. Unfortunately the conditions under which he tried to revive it had become vastly more difficult. In resources, industrial development, military organization, and the control of public opinion, Bismarck's empire was incomparably more powerful than absolutist Prussia of other days. It was more powerful also in prescribing the content and determining the aims of education. Nietzsche was fully aware of the difficulty of his position. The characterization of himself as "the last unpolitical German" sounded, in fact, like the words of a man in an outpost already hopelessly surrounded, yet resolved to make a desperate stand.

The event uppermost in the minds of Germans at the time was their military victory over the French in 1871. Nietzsche was one of the first to perceive the dangerous effects of this victory on his countrymen who were already infatuated with the technical progress they were making. The daily press and university professors alike were persuading the people to believe that the better military leadership and discipline, the greater physical endurance and more efficient organization of the Germans had proved the vitality of their culture while revealing the decadence of the French. In attacking such false self-celebration, Nietzsche for the first time dipped his pen in acid. He remonstrated with the noisy patriots that obedience, efficiency, and organization by themselves were no proof of culture, and that a combination of mass submissiveness and technical preoccupation was in fact on the way to "extirpating German genius in favor of the German Reich." [3] Creative imagination and individuality, he said, were being crushed by engineers, drill sergeants, and patriotic professors. Thus, he began to despise the Germany which reveled in technology, parades, and pointless erudition.

One of his first specific attacks was leveled at the newly rich and at the German bourgeoisie who seemed to him the bearers of what he derisively termed "this modern culture." He blamed the indiscriminate and sudden rush of this class at education for the general depression of taste and intelligence. Crude social ambitions and smugness over material affluence, he charged, were producing a priggish, obtuse type of person for whom he coined the term *Bildungsphilister*. What most appalled him in this German Babbitt was the absence of sincerity and ideal interests. Culture was becoming a label for respectability and a veneer with which to disguise a paltry life. It was treated as a relaxation from the "seriousness of life" by which, Nietzsche said, the Philistine meant his work, house, wife, and children. If he sent his sons to higher schools, bought the classics, and went to concerts, he did so for the wrong reasons: he wished to be "elevated," to rest his nerves and aid his digestion. Whatever the motives of the Philistine's patronage of culture, his listlessness and affection were sterilizing influences.[4]

Nietzsche thought it necessary to tell these Babbitts some unpalatable truths. Education, he reminded them, could not be bought with money and ambition. It was an achievement of disciplining oneself by examples and visions of human excellence, and only a minority of high-minded individuals were capable of it at any time, regardless of the illusions of progress that a period might entertain. Education was a matter of forming relationships with a few great minds, not for the purpose of idle hero worship, but to find in them the very sources of all that is rare and noble in human life. Self-discipline, then, was a sense of individual responsibility for maintaining in one's own

CRITICISM AND SATIRE OF ACADEMIC CULTURE

person the humanist tradition and the standards set by an elite. Unlike Fichte, however, Nietzsche was not a moralizing puritan. He placed the emphasis, as an artist would, on form, grace, precision, and clarity. Education was self-formation in all these respects, crowned by the achievement of a unified style of life and integration of all one's powers into a creative whole.[5] It is a conception of education chiefly reminiscent of Humboldt and Goethe. It was the indifference of German academic science and scholarship to this ideal of education and, as the following pages will show, their lack of philosophical reflection and depth that provoked Nietzsche's criticism.

In the discussion that follows, the most important ideas contained in his criticism are organized under three main heads:

(1) In an advanced stage of academic specialization the broader problems of culture and education meet with indifference on the part of the universities. The professor becomes a parody of the educated man.

(2) Culture depends upon more than purely rational intelligence. Excessive rationalism is intolerant and destructive of creative thought which springs from irrational sources.

(3) In an Alexandrine age those who collect, discover, and record specific information are deemed, and deem themselves, superior to those who create, reflect, and educate. Education is confused with accumulation and mastery of steadily growing amounts of subject matter. Specialists usurp the rank of philosophers and educators.

(1)

David Friedrich Strauss (1808–1874), whom Nietzsche chose as the target of his satire on Philistinism, was a scholar whose main work had been in the application of the methods of historical criticism to the history of Christian dogma and to the life of Christ. This interest, and the courage of publishing his findings in the face of orthodox vested interests—professorships at the Universities of Zürich and Tübingen were lost to him as a result—had given the man the reputation of being a "progressive." Late in his life Strauss made capital of this reputation by publishing *The Old Faith and the New* (1872), in which he expanded his "progressive" scholarship into a "progressive" faith in modern life. He there confessed that he could no longer consider himself a Christian, and added that this should in fact have become impossible for any intellectual in sympathy with "modern developments." As a substitute for Christianity Strauss offered a new faith which in effect was an incongruous mixture of loyalties and beliefs. He endorsed the national power state, free private enterprise, the world view of nineteenth-century science, the advancement of material welfare, and the expansion of public education, to which was added a Philistine appreciation of the German classics in music and literature. The following is a sample of the culture of modernity.

"Let us just indicate how we do it and have been doing it for many years. In addition to our profession—and we belong to all sorts of professions, for we are by no means only scholars or artists, but also officials and officers, businessmen and landholders, and once more, as already mentioned, there are not a few of us but many thousand and not the worst in the land—besides our profession, I say, we try to keep our minds open, as much as possible, for all the higher interests of mankind: we have during the last years taken active part in the great national war and in the establishment of a unified German state, and we feel supremely elevated by this turn in the fate, as unexpected as it is glorious, of our much tried nation. We aid our understanding of these events by historical studies which have now been made easy, even for the untutored, by means of a series of attractively and popularly written historical works; we also seek to broaden our knowledge of nature, for which purpose popular aids of study are not wanting either; and, finally, we find in the writings of our great poets, in the performances of the works of our great musicians, a stimulation for mind and soul, for imagination and humor which leaves nothing to be desired. Thus we live, thus we saunter happily." [6]

Perhaps Nietzsche would not have taken any notice of Strauss had it not been for the astonishing success of the book.[7] *The Old Faith and the New* was soon accepted as a sort of cultural guide by the German middle classes, including university circles to whom the author primarily addressed him-self. Apart from Strauss's critical scholarship, Nietzsche found nothing admirable in his life and nothing meaningful in his thought, and as the philosopher of flabby modernity Strauss repelled him. Nietzsche showed that the modern faith, with which Strauss gave himself such an air, was nothing but the sum of current social prejudices and the quintessence of vulgarity. The interpretation of German classics which Strauss gave in his book was embarrassing, for it only revealed to Nietzsche the author's own banality. His style of writing, for which Nietzsche took him severely to task, was affected and studded with clichés and trivialities. How, Nietzsche asked himself, could such a testament of mediocrity make an impression on so-called educated people and especially on the academic profession?

In answering for the latter group, whose pathology he was then beginning to write, Nietzsche explained that the academic specialist applies all his energy and thought to a narrowly restricted field of labor which he isolates from the common ground. There he works dutifully and "hard." After a series of exhausting days and nights spent in what he is pleased to call the pursuit of truth, his tired nerves demand relaxation from the monotony of his labors. In this respect he behaves, Nietzsche said, like the most unfortunate members of mankind, those who have become the slaves of their occupation or their material needs. Like theirs, the scholar's life is no longer integrated. Duty and pleasure are divorced from each other and the two halves, pursued separately, frustrate the achievement of an integrated personality. The modern scholar and scientist, he said, do not know the ancient meaning of "leisure." They have also forgotten, he indicated, that good teaching becomes impossible when sensitivity to human relationships is blunted. He was even more disturbed by the specialist's evasion of general cultural responsibility and the atrophy of his power of judgment. Such decadence frightened Nietzsche all the more because it seemed to be unnoticed by the decadents themselves.

The main reason why university people accepted Strauss as an authority in matters of culture, he thought, was that Strauss succeeded in reassuring them that cultural leadership was still found in their circles. Here was a scholar and a specialist who had undertaken to survey and interpret the whole of contemporary culture, an effort they admired. For how few of them were still willing or able to do this? Moreover, they trusted his scholarship, which they confused with judgment, and they were thus inclined to accept his dicta on what to believe, what to like, and how to orient themselves in a rapidly changing world. Without their noticing it, Nietzsche said, the academic profession and the academically educated had sunk to the level of Philistines. They did not realize the pretensions and priggishness in Strauss. They did not notice that "the highest interests of mankind," of which he spoke, conflicted with nationalist "elevation"; that "businessmen and landowners" need not necessarily be the noblest representatives of the human race; or that wealth and culture are not necessarily related. It was this academic fragment of humanity that provoked from Nietzsche the following famous caricature.

"This paradox, the scholar-scientist (der wissenschaftliche Mensch), has recently become so harassed in Germany that it appears as if science and learning were a factory in which even a few minutes' tardiness imposes punishments. He works as hard as the fourth, or slave, caste. His studies are no longer an occupation but a necessity. He looks neither to the right nor the left and passes through all matters and concerns of life with that half measure of alertness, that need for relaxation so characteristic of the exhausted laborer. This also determines his relation to culture. . . . Even in his dreams he cannot throw off his yoke—just like a slave who still in his freedom dreams of his misery, his haste, and his beating. . . . Now Pascal thinks that men pursue their business and their sciences with such single-mindedness in order to escape the most important questions which every moment of loneliness and true leisure would urge upon them—questions concerning the Why, Whence, and Whither of life. But, curiously enough, not even the most obvious question occurs to our scholars: what benefit their labor, their haste, and their painful ecstasies can possibly have? . . . But if, as men of science, you go about science in the same manner in which workers go about the tasks which life's daily necessities impose upon them, then what is to become of a culture condemned to await the hour of its birth and its salvation amidst this excited, breathless, aimless, fidgeting infatuation with science and learning? Nobody can spare any time for culture, and yet what meaning is there in any science and learning at all, if it has no time for culture? Answer this one, at least: whence, whither, and why all science if it is not meant to lead to culture? Perhaps, then, to barbarism! Already we see the learned class advanced appallingly far in this direction, if one may believe that such superficial books as that of Strauss do justice to its present state of culture. For exactly there do we meet that repulsive need of rest and that casual, half-attentive coming-to-terms with philosophy and culture and the seriousness of human existence. One is reminded of the social gatherings of the learned which, once the shop talk has ceased, testify only to fatigue, to the desire for distraction at any price, to a ravaged memory, and to an incoherent experience of life. . . .

"The only form of culture which the inflamed eye and the dulled brain of the learned working class can tackle is that *Philistine culture* whose gospel Strauss has proclaimed. . . . That culture carries the expression of contentment in its face and does not want any changes in the present state of German education. It is above all seriously convinced of the superiority of all German educational institutions, especially of the Gymnasia and the universities. It does not cease recommending them warmly to foreign countries and it doubts not for a moment that Germany has become, through them, the nation which

is most educated and has the greatest capacity of judgment.
. . . Second, it commits the last judgment in all questions of
culture and taste to the authority of scholars and regards itself
as the ever-growing repository of learned opinions on art, literature, and philosophy. Its concern is to urge the learned man to
express his opinions and then to administer them, in a mixed
or simplified form, as a potion to the German people." [8]

From *Beyond Good and Evil* another passage on Nietzsche's
pathology of the academic man is added:

"When compared to genius—a being which begets and brings
forth—the scholar and average scientific man have something
in common with the old maid: like her they are incapable of
the two most valuable functions of man. By way of compensation one grants respectability to both the scholar and the old
maid. . . . Looked at more closely, what sort of man is the
scholar? In the first place, he is a common type of man with
the virtues of that type, that is, he is neither authoritative nor
self-sufficient. He is industrious, submerges himself patiently in
the rank and file, and is moderate in his ability and his demands.
He has the instinct for what is necessary to his kind: for example,
that amount of independence and green pasture without which
there is no peace for work; those claims to honor and recognition . . . , the sunshine which radiates from a good reputation; and that constant affirmation of his worth and usefulness
with which the inner distrust, at the bottom of the hearts of
all unfree men and herd animals, must again and again be over-
come. As is only natural, the scholar also has the infirmities
and bad manners of the vulgar sort of man. He is rich in petty
envy and looks lynx-eyed for blemishes in all characters who
have reached heights he can never attain." [9]

This was brilliant writing and a fine piece of imaginative
psychology. That it was also largely true, those on the inside of
academic life know best. Certainly the type analyzed is today far from becoming extinct. Of course, the professorial
deformities and the debilitating character of academic work
were portrayed by Nietzsche not without malice and caricatural

delight. There were, however, a few contemporaries of his who taught in the universities and to whom he also could have pointed as humane and imaginative teachers and scholars. Two such men, Jacob Burckhardt and Wilhelm Dilthey, are mentioned in the latter part of this chapter. Through their work they imparted new life and significance to the humanities, and though both were critical of German higher learning, their criticism was not, like Nietzsche's, destructive. On the other hand, the aimless, bewildered, and pathetic type whom Nietzsche castigated was all too numerous. Two figures, Wilamovitz and Diels, are later offered as illustrations, and they provide specific evidence for the justice of Nietzsche's criticism. But first it is necessary to show how this deprecation of the professor and the intellectual had its root in his own irrationalist philosophy of culture.

(2)

Nietzsche first speculated on the meaning of culture in *The Birth of Tragedy*, a youthful and, as he himself admitted in the Preface of 1886, an "impossible" piece of work. Yet, with all its immaturity, this essay probed into a series of momentous problems. One of these was to determine which kind of human achievement was of greatest value in what he called the vitality of culture.

Nietzsche contrasted two major kinds of cultural achievement: rationalist thought, under which he included science and scholarship, and certain transcendental forms of art. To illustrate the cultural values of each, he turned to the history of ancient Greek and modern German civilization, between which his essay attempted to draw certain parallels. He found the greatest expressions of metaphysical art in Greek tragedy and Wagnerian music, especially *Tristan and Isolde*. The climax of rationalist thought, on the other hand, he placed in Socratic philosophy and nineteenth-century science and scholarship, but added that each of these triumphs had had destructive effects on cultural growth. Scholars, scientists, and theorists flourished, so he generalized, in periods of cultural decline, characterized by rank exuberance of analytic and pragmatic thought which, he maintained, stifled the imagination and the creative urge.

This was clearly a radical simplification of a difficult problem, and perhaps the problem itself was falsely stated. Nietzsche also arrived at dangerous half-truths which certain irrationalist vitalists of the twentieth century seized upon in order to undermine, preparatory to Nazism itself, trust in rational judgment and criticism.[10] Of chief interest here, however, is his valuation of *Wissenschaft*, by which he meant rational thought and science. To estimate the value of *Wissenschaft*, he argued, it was necessary to ascertain whether it deepened or conventionalized, enlarged or narrowed man's understanding of himself and the nature of human existence in general. His answer to this problem was unorthodox and singular. In striking agreement with Kierkegaard, whose anti-rationalism is discussed in the next chapter, Nietzsche maintained that the rational world constructed by science, logic, and critical scholarship was fundamentally an artificial world. It was incongruous with the tragic existence which, to his mind, was man's real world. The rational artificial world, he suspected, was becoming a refuge and a mechanism of escape for those who were afraid to face the irrational and tragic qualities of human life, which in the end always remained unescapable. That there actually were scientists who denied these qualities, just as they denied the existence of problems which their methods did not allow them to solve, was demonstrated at the end of the last chapter. The naïve optimism and the dogmatism of such scientists as Haeckel and Ostwald are the best illustrations of the limitations Nietzsche was talking about.

Now the point he made was that no vital culture could grow out of such a contrived rationalism. To grow at all, culture required as its indispensable condition that man know and accept existence as it really is, with all its frenzies, anxieties, and senseless suffering. To affirm life, despite the knowledge that its meaning is problematic, demanded a tragic and a heroic sense. And lest this knowledge overwhelm and crush man, it was necessary that he express it through means of art. Artists capable of achieving this were therefore most vital to the very existence of a mature culture, and vastly more important than scholars and scientists. Tragic art—that is, art derived from a tragic conception of life—was not an evasion. It was man's victory over the dark fearfulness of life and gave him freedom.

The autobiographical flavor in this discussion of the limitations of rationalism is unmistakable. Ever since Nietzsche had, as a student, discovered Schopenhauer's major work, he had been persuaded that the most powerful and creative elements of human life were irrational. His inner estrangement from the modes of thought prevalent in academic circles perhaps dated from that time. During his several years in Basle, his great admiration for Wagner was another and more intense experience which diminished his taste for the scholar's life and gave new inspiration to his philosophy. *The Birth of Tragedy*, actually a rhapsody on Wagner, was the clearest presage of Nietzsche's own destiny. He desired even then the risks, the passion, and the freedom of the mind's greater battles which, he was convinced, were no longer fought in universities. *The Birth of Tragedy* anticipated the more radical polemical writings of the 1880's when, in addition to the professor and the rationalist, he denounced as deficient and fragmentary types such men as the Christian, the humanitarian, and the democratic liberal because they denied and effaced themselves and their life was common, meek, unheroic, and untragic. But by that time the vision of the superman had come to rule his mind.

(3)

In his criticism of the work of universities Nietzsche was generally less concerned with science than with the humanities about which he could speak with a greater degree of competence. History especially he subjected to a detailed criticism in

The Use and Abuse of History. There he complained about the general confusion of history with antiquarianism, and the inorganic accumulation of factual information with education. Though himself a classicist by training and early profession, he charged that classical education had become identical with historical-philological drill and drudgery and was enfeebling the minds of young people. Similar charges of overtaxing the mental powers of pupils were brought, notably against the Prussian Gymnasia, also by other critics.[11] He objected further against the German tendency to borrow and imitate foreign culture, which hardly provided a thin veneer for the crudeness of modern Imperial Germany. Culture grew only from original experiences and visions, not from the perfunctory acquisition of historical knowledge *about* culture. He went further and encouraged the better part of German youth to rebel against the imposition of such veneer and against the stifling pedantry of the philologists and historians. He thought that the time had come for drastic measures against the sterility of German education.

The chief cause for the uncontrolled expansion of this sterile historical erudition was, according to Nietzsche, the false conception of history as a science. Historical scholars pretended to be able to furnish "objective" knowledge about the past. Since Ranke, they had hoped to reproduce the past photographically, as it were, on the sensitized plates of the present, and the plates were they themselves. To put it in Nietzsche's own words: the objective man "waits until something comes along and then spreads himself out tenderly, so that not even the lightest footfalls of ghostlike beings slipping past shall be lost upon his surface." [12] He protested that history was neither passive nor objective. On the contrary, it consisted of acts of understanding and evaluation performed by human beings who, if they were truly alive, had purposes and ideals of their own. For this reason, he said, the study of history was necessarily selective. Periods and nations with a strong sense of their own mission and importance, he added, have unerringly recognized this. They preferred, as he put it, monumental to antiquarian history. In other words, history with them was frankly educational in the sense that it was the study of models and examples inspiring and encouraging to the living.

Nietzsche analyzed this belief in "objectivity" and found that it contained a number of scholarly foibles and vices. In the first place, "objectivity" seemed to him to be a euphemism for the inability of the rank and file of scholars to distinguish between things important and things unimportant. "Objective" scholars made a virtue out of this incapacity by calling irrelevancy or platitudinousness, impartiality. Second, failure to define their criteria of importance permitted them to protract their labors without ever coming to a conclusion. It afforded them the happiness of permanent employment and of concealing from themselves the futility of their efforts and their life. Third, "objectivity" was a misnomer for indifference to philosophy. The common variety of historiographer seemed to think that his work would produce pure, "objective" knowledge if from the very start he was completely detached from the object of his inquiry. Detachment, however, Nietzsche said, was not an endowment but a philosophical achievement of minds who learned to scrutinize themselves. Fourth and finally, the great crowd of historiographers were ordinary fellows who shared the conventions and fables of their age. But because they were uncritical, they mistook conformity to public opinion for established standards of truth. The patriotic Prussian professors of history, referred to in the first chapter, of course did not pretend to be objective, and Nietzsche scorned *them* for their nationalistic conceit.

With this pitiless analysis of the scholarly small fry Nietzsche did not mean to assert that objective truth was worthless or nonexistent. Later it is true, he did say that falsehood, if it prove life-preserving, may be preferable to truth, and even this youthful essay contained intimations of the dangers of an unhistorical conception of life. Yet he was also being constructive: the point he wished to make was that to write history required passionate interest in one's subject, a sense of intellectual responsibility, and, most important, a philosophy of history. For without that the study of history was meaningless. Nietzsche, however, was not himself a historian, and in order to estimate better the weight of his criticism, it is worth while introducing at this point some pertinent opinions of two important historians, Jacob Burckhardt and Wilhelm Dilthey. Contemporaries of Nietzsche, both were unorthodox, imaginative scholars, sharply critical of academic positivism, interested in the philosophy and methodology of history, and, as humanists, concerned with reestablishing the study of history as an essential part of liberal education.

Burckhardt, a citizen of Basle and Nietzsche's elder colleague at the University, was little known or respected during his lifetime (1818–1897). His reputation did not begin to grow until after his death, and it has in fact grown most remarkably during the last decade when people began to discover in his letters uncanny predictions of the present world catastrophe.[13] Burckhardt's lack of popularity during the nineteenth century was due in large measure to the fact that, like Nietzsche, he rebelled against the prevalent type of historical scholarship. With quite sovereign confidence in his own standard of values he ignored all pressure and enticement to conform to the academic cliques of professional historiographers in Germany. Though trained there and filled with admiration for its older cultural traditions, those antedating 1848, Burckhardt regarded German academic and political life after 1870 with mixed feelings of scorn and anxiety.

As for the study of history, he saw his task not in erudition and research, but in the interpretation of selected periods of Western civilization. "A quite remarkable phenomenon has become clear to me as a teacher of history," he wrote in 1870; "that is the sudden devaluation of all mere 'events' of the past." [14] He never deluded himself into thinking that history was something that could be "covered" by even the most arduous scholarly labors. He realized that its study must from necessity be selective. There was in him no trace of that pretense of objectivity which Nietzsche exposed. It was precluded by his frank avowals that he was interested in history only as the history of human values and that the standard which he applied in his own writings was that of a European humanist. It was natural, therefore, that he was attracted to such periods as fifth-century Greece, the Italian Renaissance, and the German Neo-humanism of Goethe and Humboldt, periods marked by individual freedom of expression in art and literature. What he cultivated and tried to make accessible to his contemporaries, whom he saw being buried under mounds of "material," was a tradition of universal human values. "We shall study," he wrote in the Introduction to the *Weltgeschichtliche Betrachtungen*, "the recurrent, constant, and typical as echoing in us and intelligible through us." Studied in this manner, history was to Burckhardt an indispensable humanizing influence, and historical piety the mark which distinguished the civilized person from the barbarian.

A friendship based on broad sympathies developed between the older historian and the budding philosopher at Basle. Both were students of classical antiquity and both admired Schopenhauer, whom Burckhardt considered the most convincing philosopher of the century. They were still more intimately united by a sense of humanist responsibility in an age becoming increasingly utilitarian, specialist, and nationalist. They protested against the degradation of education to a means of material advancement, against its ceasing to be a source of enjoyment and a self-justifying interest. Both scorned the sprawling, teeming factories of modern research and scholarship in which, as Nietzsche mocked, men behave "as if the heavens were to be stormed and the truth to be drawn from the deepest wells." [15] Burckhardt declined several invitations to large German universities, among them one to become Ranke's successor at the University of Berlin. He did not wish to be drawn into the hustle of German academic life. In a quiet town like Basle it was possible to preserve one's individuality and at the same time to enter into a wholesome civic life in which Burckhardt, as an old patrician, took great pride. Besides, Basle was a good vantage point from which to observe the changing currents in the life of Europe.

Burckhardt's indifference to "original research" irritated the scholars who took their greatest pride in it. When, for example, he published his *Griechische Kulturgeschichte*, Wilamovitz cried out—and he was joined by men like Ernst von Meyer and Julius Beloch, all three German scholars of considerable reputation: "This work does not exist for scholarship!" [16] Burckhardt remained unruffled. He had "confessed" in advance, in the Introduction, that he had neglected to use the very latest philological research. He justified this by explaining that his books were not meant to be "contributions to knowledge" and that they were not written for the specialists in the field. "Erudition," he said, "is taken care of by the current historical-antiquarian literature. We are pleading for a lifelong means of enjoyment." [17] He sounded almost as if he knew that he would be read long after the work of the specialists had become obsolete and gathered dust. Burckhardt recognized as clearly as Nietzsche the malady of the century, the neglect of education in favor of erudition and research. As a young man he had thought it shameful that after three centuries of tyrannically maintained classical education, there still did not exist one decent history of Greek culture. He had vowed to write one, and late in his life he did, knowing full well that it would not be appreciated by the *viri eruditissimi* in the German universities.

Burckhardt, who hated argument and controversy, never retaliated publicly against attacks upon him. But in letters to friends he spoke his mind about the German learned cliques. His dry, drastic comments cut perhaps more deeply than Nietzsche's satire, with which they should be read side by side. Speaking of the futility of many a scholar's labors, he said: "They begin and dig a hole. . . . Death comes meanwhile, and what do they leave us? The rubbish lying beside the hole they dug." On the crabbedness of German scholarship he commented: "The pedantry which prevails in those dim and dusty German studies is without equal. Those people no longer know that to write genuine history one must live in a subtle spiritual atmosphere, the atmosphere of art and poetry, and not merely in the source materials." Of the strictly "objective" fact collectors he wrote: "God, too, wants some fun at times, and then he creates those philologists and historians who think themselves superior to all the world when they have scientifically ascertained that the Emperor Conrad II went to the privy at Goslar on May 7 in the year 1030—and things of like world-wide interest." [18]

As already stated, Burckhardt is read today mainly because he predicted the age of totalitarianism and universal war. A brief reference to his predictions is here pertinent, for it is only within the larger political perspective that the progressive dehumanization of German education, and the anxiety with which Burckhardt and Nietzsche observed it, may be fully understood. These predictions demonstrated that the modern scholar, though he worked under the handicap of a high degree of specialization, could still unite judgment and moral sensitivity with the study of history. Burckhardt was a rare example of the educated man whose disappearance Nietzsche so deplored; he conveyed once more an idea of the full stature that the scholar could attain. The following paragraph quotes a few fragments of Burckhardt's most poignant observations:

"You cannot hope to be a culturally significant people and politically significant at the same time." "What spiritual sterility will date from the year 1870 in Germany!" "For now it is above all a question of further military preparation." "What is most serious, however, is not the present war but the *era of wars* into which we have entered." "I have a premonition which sounds like utter folly, and yet it will not leave me: the military state will become one single vast factory. Those hordes of men in the great industrial centers cannot be left indefinitely to their greed and want. What must logically come is a definite and supervised stint of misery, with promotions and uniforms, daily begun and ended to the sound of drums." "Long voluntary subjection under individual *Führers* is in prospect. People no longer believe in principles but will probably believe periodically in saviours." "My mental picture of the *terribles simplificateurs* who will overrun our old Europe is not a pleasant one." [19]

Here was tragic knowledge of the kind Nietzsche had declared wholesome and necessary. Burckhardt's prophecies obviously clashed sharply with the popular optimism advertised by certain nineteenth-century scientists such as Ostwald who had contemptuously referred to the humanities as *Papierwissenschaften*. Only half a century was required to prove that the imaginative, humanist historian who did not ape the methods of science was capable of a more universal and therefore more accurate understanding of man and the future of civilization.

Despite his pessimism, Burckhardt did not fall into moods of unrelieved despair or total radicalism. He remained active and responsible in the limited sphere of influence which he had chosen, a great teacher not only to his students at the University but to the educated citizenry of Basle. He kept his pessimism out of the classroom and could be gay and witty with his students. To the end he remained humane and humble, while Nietzsche, thirty years younger, drove himself, by his violence, into deeper and deeper isolation until he destroyed himself. Burckhardt could not share or even sympathize with the titanic aspirations of the younger man, and the more these gained power over Nietzsche's mind, the more Burckhardt's friendship cooled until he finally withdrew. Nietzsche kept sending him copies each time he published a new book. He seemed not to have noticed that a break had occurred. Burckhardt, polite and reserved as he was, never broke with him openly. But he knew that their ways had parted. At the end of the essay on *The Use and Abuse of History*, Nietzsche, out of rebellion against the sterile erudition which he felt was oppressing German education—"another century of readers and the mind itself will stink"—appealed to youth to throw off the burden of the past, even if this should mean ignorance and crudeness for a time. Burckhardt sensed the danger then. His young friend was inviting barbarism; he had begun to forsake humanism, measure, and restraint.

Wilhelm Dilthey (1833–1911), too, was little known during his lifetime. But in the twentieth century he also had an astonishing renascence, at least in Germany, and this was due in large part to his effort to redefine the meaning and structure of the humanities as distinct from science. Men such as Windelband and Rickert also shared in this effort, but their studies were limited to the narrower problems of methodology,[20] while Dilthey brought to his task a rich and subtle knowledge of history.

If one interprets rather than transcribes literally Dilthey's ideas most relevant to this discussion, one may say that his problem was to understand how, from the rich psychic flux of human life, there arises the *geistige Welt*, or that system of enduring ideal structures in art, literature, religion, and philosophy through which man, by transcending the temporary phases of existence, expresses and realizes himself. These structures, in which human values become objectified, require a mode of understanding and a method of inquiry very different from those of natural science; and this was the reason why Dilthey distinguished between science and the humanities as distinct branches of knowledge. What he called the *geistige Welt* were ideal structures which could not be "explained" in terms of mechanical causation or by reduction to uniform elements. They could only be "understood" if the historian was capable of entering imaginatively into the complex of human motives, values, conceptions, and purposes of which the culture of a period is the expression. It may seem that Dilthey relied much upon subjective empathy. Actually, he was restoring the human center of history which positivism had lost sight of, and in his often involved way he seems to be saying that we cannot understand history unless we understand ourselves. Yet again, our understanding of ourselves is enhanced as we learn to enter into the experience and the thought of others. "What man is," Dilthey wrote, "he can learn only from history." [21]

This very brief reference can do no more than indicate that had there been a majority of scholars of Dilthey's kind, the distinct and irreplaceable value of the humanities would have been better understood. Nietzsche's criticism would then have been without foundation, and he would have had no reason to demand relief from the crushing burden of a dead past. Though Dilthey's *Lebensphilosophie* was sympathetic to certain ideas of Nietzsche's, this German scholar was offended, as Burckhardt was, by Nietzsche's historical impiety and his apotheosis of the individual breaking all common ties of morality and tradition.[22]

It remains now to introduce at least some bits of positive evidence for Nietzsche's analysis of the academic man, and for this purpose two classical scholars of outstanding reputation, Wilamovitz and Diels, have been chosen. There is here no question of their scholarly achievements. Of interest are only their opinions of the larger problems of society and education. One cannot say that either of the two great scholars gave any sustained thought to such matters, although one might have expected them to. For they represented a branch of knowledge of whose superior educational importance they were convinced, and as classicists they both felt themselves the legitimate and eminent exponents of humanism. To discover what these men thought about the problems of nineteenth-century culture, one is in fact largely dependent on what escaped them in certain festive moments, as for example during academic ceremonies. With the peculiar unreality and the inflated sentiment common to such occasions, they delivered themselves of what Nietzsche aptly called their "painful ecstasies."

During his professorship at the University of Göttingen, Wilamovitz (1848–1931) delivered an address in which he proclaimed his faith in the superior values of ancient culture.[23] To preserve them, he declared, was essential for the spiritual sanity of modern Europe which he saw threatened by destructive forces. One of these was materialism which he seems to have identified with technological progress. The other, which he deemed even more dangerous, was social revolution. His fear of it, however, seems to have been prompted less by his classicism than by the fact that he was a Prussian *Junker*. There had been a period in German education when nationalism and classical humanism had excluded one another. Not so Wilamovitz, who in his *Recollections* described the German Empire and Greek culture as the two deepest concerns of his life. He was unaware of the impurity of such a belief, or of the lack of intellectual integrity which it acknowledged. With all his faults, Nietzsche was incapable of such obtuseness; in fact, he regarded it as a symptom of cultural decay.

Because of his compromising nationalism, Wilamovitz was obviously a poor spokesman for classical humanism, and perhaps his ecstatic and high-flown manner of speaking, in the address just mentioned, was an unconscious attempt to disguise the fundamental confusion of his mind. For though he had asserted the superiority of the values of antiquity, he was capable neither of saying in what they consisted, nor why and how they might be realized under modern conditions. He uttered dire warnings to Europe to let herself be saved in the last hour by the classical philologists; yet he scorned the most practical educational means available for that salvation. Wilamovitz taught in the classical department of the university in which a large number of secondary-school teachers received their academic training, and one might have expected him to begin the work of cultural reform by making humanists out of them. He asserted, however, that classical scholarship was so advanced and specialized a branch of learning that it could no longer be regarded as a means of practical humanist education. He failed to say, in support of his own thesis, what other ways remained open to the classical philologists to save the world.

But the muddle did not even end there. In the same address the great scholar advanced what sounded like a reasonable argument, namely, that the decline of Greek antiquity was caused by social and political conflicts and that neither artistic nor philosophical greatness could have prevented it. Yet this argument seemed not to have the slightest influence upon his extravagant belief that the decline of modern Europe could be arrested by the revival of classical literature. To this belief Wilamovitz clung with the desperate unreasonableness of a child. He confessed himself much encouraged by the fact that in several Western nations societies for the advancement of Greek philology were being established, and at the end of his address he cried: "If only we are faithful to our ideal, we shall look the coming century firmly in the eye. Whatever it may bring the nations, the sun of Homer, magnificent as on the first day, will shine over the wide world, giving light and life to the souls of men." In the face of such a quagmire of ideas, it is difficult not to agree with Nietzsche's pathology of the academic man.

Hermann Diels (1848–1922), best known for his work on the Pre-Socratic philosophers, is another illustration. Diels once wrote an article on the etymology of the term "element," [24] with which he honored a scholar friend on his sixtieth birthday. The friend was engaged in the preparation of a large Latin dictionary, and Diels wrote him that he was happy to make a contribution, but apologized for its being such a modest one—his article ran to a mere eighty-seven pages. He also confessed to his friend that much as he appreciated a great Latin dictionary, the compilation of a *thesaurus graecus* was in his opinion of still greater importance. Because of the greater richness of the Greek language, it would require a work whose size Diels estimated at ten times the volume of the Latin thesaurus and its cost at six million marks. He was dismayed, temporarily at least, by the problem of raising so large an amount of money. For was not scientific research devouring most of the funds, and was not the scientific infatuation of academic youth still growing? Some day, however, science and technology would cease to be fads, and modern man, disillusioned, would return to drink deeply from the well of ancient culture. It was necessary to have faith and hold on to the ideal dictionary until—here for some obscure reason Diels lapsed into Biblical language—"the time would be fulfilled" when such a work would rise like a gigantic monument "on an international basis," financed by an idealistic youth from all over the world. Thus the classicist faltered and sadly neglected his true office.

There is a diary which records a student's impressions of some of the great scholars at the University of Berlin around 1900. It was written by an eager and sensitive young man who, already after a few semesters, turned away disillusioned from academic learning which, in the title of his diary, he called *Die Wissenschaft des Nichtwissenswerten.*[25] Most of his criticism of the professors whose lectures, seminars, and homes he visited coincides with that of Nietzsche, so that there is no need of recording it here. Only one remark is worth repeating. Diels, so the young writer said, had taken it upon himself to denounce Nietzsche for his mania of the superman. He confessed that he was puzzled. For what after all, he asked, was the vision of the superman as compared with the ecstasy of a superlexicographer?

* * *

The hope of revitalizing German academic education, which had originally inspired his critical essays, Nietzsche soon abandoned. Already in the third part of *Thoughts Out of Season*, entitled *Schopenhauer as Educator* (1874), he decided that German universities and higher schools were beyond repair and that radically new educational institutions and values must be created. He then began to form the idea of a new elite about which the social order was to crystallize. At that time Schopenhauer represented to him the type of intellectual leadership which was needed. What drew Nietzsche to him and what he admired in Schopenhauer was that philosopher's fight against the accredited forms of academic philosophy and his resistance to the rule of mediocrity and democracy.[26] The new elite was apparently to be constituted by academic outsiders and social rebels who would found small schools or sects of devoted disciples. But Nietzsche never developed this idea. Instead he began to speak of the new aristocracy in terms of animal strength and breeding, biological fitness, and military power. Even this naturalistic vocabulary did not make his vision clear. He knew well enough what he scorned and hated. The "will to power," however, remained a protest and the expression of no more than an impulse to escape human mediocrity. It was, on the one hand, a renewal of romantic German striving, and on the other a presage of new and powerful instincts yet to be unfettered. Nietzsche did not enlighten the future; he became its ferment.

CHAPTER V

THE GROWTH OF MODERN IRRATIONALISM AND FASCIST MYTHOLOGY

Because of its literary, paradoxical, and fragmentary quality, and because his was an aphoristic rather than a systematic philosophy, Nietzsche's thought was not well suited to being transmitted and developed in the form of a "school." Yet there was hardly a German thinker or educationist who ignored Nietzsche, as there was hardly an educated man who did not read him and was not excited by him. Under these circumstances, it is difficult to define his great influence in the 1890's and in the first two decades of the twentieth century more precisely than by saying that it formed a characteristic ingredient of the intellectual atmosphere of that period. The melancholy remark of Hegel that he had one disciple and that he was misunderstood by that one, is applicable with even greater truth to Nietzsche. To diverse minds with contrary theses to prove and diverse axes to grind, his writings offered equally rich opportunities. Everyone now knows, for example, that both Nazis and anti-Nazis made it a practice to supply themselves with quotations from his work.

It is, therefore, with some arbitrariness that a number of writers have here been singled out and labeled Nietzscheans. It can be said, however, that these men were the most persuasive spokesmen of ideas, sentiments, and *ressentiments* either directly borrowed from, or inspired by, Nietzsche. They include writers from the end of the nineteenth century to the Nazi philosophers Alfred Baeumler and Ludwig Klages, all of whom fed and elaborated upon Nietzsche's criticism of culture and education. Even among these Nietzscheans sharp disagreements and animosities persisted. The circle around the poet Stefan George, for example, had esthetic and humanist aspirations which, as in Nietzsche himself, were expressed in defiance of the conditions of the modern world. Spengler, on the other hand, seized upon the idea of the will to power and, by oversimplifying it, made of it a weapon for military and technological survival. But in spite of their differences, all of these Nietzscheans caught the contagion of a mood of mind in which rebelliousness, cynicism, and the readiness to damn were uppermost, and in which destructive criticism and the sterile excitement of romantics triumphed in the end over the spirit of serious reform.

Educational interest broadened considerably in Germany toward the end of the century when, in 1890 and in 1900, two school conferences were called by the Emperor in Berlin, the latter resulting in important changes in the secondary school system, among them one depriving the Gymnasium of its monopoly in pre-university training. The educational agitation and criticism which preceded and accompanied these conferences helped to pave the way for the success of two authors who made the reform of German schools and of German culture, no less, their business.

Of the two, Paul de Lagarde (1827–1891) was a well-known Orientalist at the University of Göttingen, a man of considerable educational experience also in the Gymnasium, and in some respects at least an informed and serious critic. The other, Julius Langbehn (1851–1907), was a man of private life and an impossible dilettante who knew little of anything. But it was Langbehn who achieved by far the greater success. His book *Der Rembrandtdeutsche* (1890) had forty editions in less than three years. It had a certain revival after World War I and reached its sixtieth edition in 1925. The book, which has not been translated into English, has no merit of any kind, it is the shoddiest of literary wares. It is, however, significant as a self-revelation of that peculiarly German brand of pretentious and ambitious vulgarity which Nietzsche had castigated but which only now began to run wild. To compare David Friedrich

Strauss, whom Nietzsche had so mercilessly exposed as the epitome of culture Philistinism, to Langbehn would be grossly flattering to the author of *Der Rembrandtdeutsche*. This author, far from being restrained by Nietzsche's criticism, boldly appropriated certain of his ideas. German education, so ran the gist of his foolish book, had overburdened the intellect, had destroyed the power of judgment and lamed the will to action. Langbehn saw personified in Rembrandt the educational ideal which was to help German youth extract itself from the cold embrace of reason and knowledge. Rembrandt meant passion, intuition, vitality, and genius, and he seemed all the more attractive because of his "German ancestry" which Langbehn—in the manner in which the Nazis later made Shakespeare a German —found no difficulty in establishing. Here are a few relevant passages for the reader's instruction and amusement:

"In the name 'Rembrandt' itself lies a very special breath of individuality. . . . His name is almost as rare as his art. This fact is full of significance, namely, that not only spirit and body, but also names and things stand in a strange secret relation to each other." "Dust is a dry food, the learned men should not eat too much of it. They should take their example from Rembrandt's art, the most melting and therefore in a sense the wettest art that has ever existed." "The Professor is the German national disease; present education of German youth is a kind of Bethlehem child murder." "Above all, false objectivity must be fought against. Cold-bloodedness is useful, but frogs, too, have cold blood. Yet the frog's perspective is not therefore the right one from which to judge the world." "The modern German will have to choose between 'man' and 'professor.' " "The specialist has surrendered his soul, yes, one may say that the devil is a specialist just as surely as God is a universalist. . . . That is, fewer eyeglasses and microscopes, and more eye and heart is what the modern German needs. . . . The German historical past has to be treated . . . as an educational institution for the future." "The heart-lifting wisdom which proclaims that intuition is higher than knowledge and which, in so far as all faith is intuition, may also be described as religious wisdom, is above all an artistic wisdom. The tie between art and religion is . . . not merely external. Both look to the whole, and that is why science is to them hostile and inferior. What might be called a science of subjective impressions could form a bridge, as it were, leading from the realm of knowledge to the realm of faith. Knowledge produces only pigmies, but faith produces heroes." [1]

These statements, delivered in perfect seriousness, constitute one of the best anticipations of the Nazi conception of education. One discerns the willful romanticism and the voluptuous itch to let oneself go in nihilist rebellion. One sees emerge here the contempt for understanding and for the patience necessary to deal with the growing complexity of modern life, the refusal to think things through and the abandonment to unqualified emotions. Langbehn's is the first popular document of incitement to national irresponsibility. Yet his contemporaries, with negligible exceptions, found nothing ominous in him, not even in the anti-Semitism which formed so smooth a union with his nationalism. Standard German encyclopedias in pre-Hitler editions describe Langbehn as the sincere prophet of a new inwardness and idealism and, of all things, as the courageous opponent of *Halbbildung*.[2] Langbehn, his damage done, died in peace and a convert to Catholicism.

A decade later, several foreign writers appeared for the first time in German, historians whom the Nazis were to acclaim as the true ancestors of their theory of the cultural superiority of the Aryan race. Chief among these were Houston Stewart Chamberlain whose *Grundlagen des 19. Jahrhunderts* was first published in 1899 and Count Gobineau whose *Essai sur l'inégalité des races humaines* was first translated into German in four volumes in 1898–1901. At about that time, too, several of Carlyle's works, including his lectures *On Heroes and Hero-Worship*, began to be read in Germany. I do not underestimate the responsibility of these men—all of whom, with the exception of Carlyle, achieved greater popularity in Germany than in

their native countries—for the growth of views and opinions
menacing to the existence of a common European culture. But
since their destructive work has lately received much attention,
I feel justified in merely mentioning them here and passing on
to Oswald Spengler who, two decades after Langbehn, caused
another sensation in 1918 with the first volume of *The Decline
of the West*.

The gulf which divides Langbehn from Spengler is as wide
as the gulf between ignorance and knowledge, quackery and
diagnosis. Yet the current which carried them both was the
same irrationalism, and in Spengler, it gained in depth and
power. A critique of Spengler the historian and the philosopher
of history is beyond the pale of this study. Attention is here
being called to Spengler the educator, the man who, far from
content with being the prophet of history, craved also to be
its agent. In his major work these two roles are blended into
one, so that it would be difficult to analyze the one without the
other. Once *The Decline of the West* was completed, however,
Spengler's theoretical interest was exhausted and he began, in
numerous minor writings and addresses, to play a frankly
political role in Germany. To dissuade German youth from
democracy then became one of his major aims. His voice, however, did not reach all. With all his vilifications of the mind,
Spengler was an intellectual and no leader of the masses. He
succeeded in casting his spell over certain sections of German
academic youth, especially those of petty middle-class back-
ground who, bewildered and fear-ridden, no longer had any
roots in the older humanist tradition. For it was these—of whom,
by the way, Heinrich Hauser in *The German Talks Back* (1945)
has furnished America with an excellent example [3]—who found
Spengler irresistible and who, at the expense of moral paralysis,
submitted to his conception of history as an inevitable natural
process.

Spengler renewed the war of instinct, feeling, and intuition
against the intellect. Langbehn's romantic desire to fuse science,
art, and religion, à la Wagner, into a single form of knowledge

also motivated Spengler. Analytic thought, he said, was the blight of the creative mind, and causal thinking was not suited to history. He scorned pragmatic and dialectic hypotheses as much as he feared them, for they destroyed the "secret," the "fateful" and "organic" character with which he dogmatically endowed history. He made capital of the words "time" and "destiny." "No hypothesis, no science can ever get into touch with that which we feel when we let ourselves sink into the meaning and sound of these words." [4] The historian, according to him, required a special sensibility which was a compound of thought and feeling, a *Denksinnlichkeit*, as one of his contemporaries named it. Spengler emphasized that this sensibility was not acquired or learned in universities. The great historian and the statesman were born to their respective forms of mastery.

In the second volume of *The Decline of the West*, which was far less a sensation than the first, Spengler showed his hand more openly. Personal resentments overcame him there with strange suddenness. There is a badly concealed anger in the assertion that genuine history is not cultural history, that, on the contrary, it is to be discovered only in the struggle for racial survival, and in war and diplomacy which are its means. Struggle and war always prevail between the sexes and generations as well as between nations. "War is the creator of all great things," [5] and in its rhythm men constantly aim to defend and to destroy each other. There is harshness and sadism in the similar assertion that "in the historical world there are no ideals, but only facts —no truths, but only facts." [6] What caused this anger was precisely the existence of universal human values, of impulses of generosity and sacrifice, such as are contained in Christianity and humanism which he found too difficult to account for. Spengler lost control of himself in alternately denying and denouncing those values so uncomfortable to his history and his politics. Any education which attempted to mold the individual in accordance with those values, in his eyes mere waste products of history, was to him either hypocritical or futile. In the case of modern Germany especially, educational ideals of that sort were a crime for they thwarted the nation in its attempt to regain political and industrial power in the world. There was in Spengler's philosophy, so strange a mixture of positivism, soothsaying, and aggressiveness, no place for *Bildung*. By none of the German irrationalists was humanism more deeply resented. There was no longer even a word about the individual and the liberation of his creative powers. Education to Spengler was simply *Zucht*, biological and social breeding for unquestioning conformity and acceptance of the national "destiny" such as the great statesman, with the help of the great historian, saw fit to proclaim and decree.

German schools and universities did not find favor with Spengler. Though their Christianity and their humanism had in fact been well adulterated, higher education was for him too intellectual and too artificial to produce the elite which the resurgence of German national strength seemed to him to make necessary. He admired the noble breeding of the medieval courtly tradition, such as he conceived it to have been, and the modern English Public Schools which, in his opinion, trained men's unreflective discipline but also their will to domination. It was the nineteenth-century Anglo-Saxon world, not Germany, which had produced the type of man whom he recommended as a model: Cecil Rhodes, for example, and even the American millionaire, ruthless and efficient men without illusions. Germany, so he warned her youth, had had her poets and philosophers; her spiritual resources were exhausted. Of course, the Anglo-Saxon nations, too, had entered the autumnal phase of their existence, but their will to domination had not yet died. To strain in order to match them should be Germany's ambition. But to realize that, it was first necessary to destroy that handful of revolutionary scoundrels who, in 1918, had forced Germany into peace and democracy, to wipe out that national disgrace and to begin to learn to hate once more. For "who cannot hate is not a man, and history is made by men." [7] It was time to stop listening to the seductive babble of humanitarians and pacifists, wasting one's attention upon the "metropolitan" literati and the perversions of modernistic art. "Art," Spengler cried, "yes, but in concrete and steel. Poetry, yes, but by men of iron nerves and merciless profundity. . . . Politics, yes, but by statesmen and not by world-reformers." [8]

Thus one discovers in these later political writings almost primitive emotions of hatred and fear, the expression of which increased in brutality until it reached a climax in *Man and Technics* (1931). There one reads of Spengler's fear of the eventual loss of white supremacy in the world brought about by a receding Western imperialism weakened at home by humanitarian ideas and the threat of "mutiny" by the laboring masses; of the loss of nerve on the part of the industrial and military leadership of the West; of the loss of pre-eminence of Western science, technology, and finance to the Orient which may finally destroy the West by ruinous economic competition. Such fears and resentments were not unfamiliar in Western countries in general, or in the Western bourgeoisie in particular. But in Germany, where in consequence of a lost war and a radical inflation, the bourgeoisie was threatened with extinction, those emotions were particularly intense. Spengler was one of the last spokesmen of that desperate class, whose sons and daughters, in the struggle for economic survival, began to overcrowd German universities in the 1920's. Perhaps that best explains the appeal which he had to academic youth at that time. It may be objected that he created a following primarily by his analyses and by the gloom of a prognosis the threat of which is more oppressive today than when it was first made, and that it is as unfair as it is futile to condemn the man's work by a revelation of his mean prejudices. The reply, it seems to me, is that Spengler's deepest insights sprang from his kinship with the forces of domination, exploitation, and suppression in history, and in so far as these continue to prevail in the modern world, to that extent Spengler's prognosis will remain valid. [9]

No other German helped as much as Spengler to create in Germany that fatal mood in which many, not wholly unintelligent, people saw a course of desperate and irrational action as the only alternative to cravenly resigning themselves to an obscure place in history. He was counsel to the history soon to be in the making, and his service to that was considerable. But toward the end of the twenties he began to lose ground to the Nazis in his influence on youth. He did not become a Nazi and had the courage to say so. There were several differences between the two, but they make little difference now. In the end, Spengler reacted to the stark reality of brute power as had also Nietzsche, whom he so admired for having been the first great German to summon his people to seize their "destiny," politically and militarily.[10] In one of his last mad letters written from Turin in 1889, Nietzsche, having hitched the future of the race to the Cesare Borgias, showed himself outraged by the much less ruthless Bismarck and William II whom, together with "all anti-Semites," he threatened to liquidate. So Spengler is supposed to have said before his death that he hoped the Pope —strange quarters for him to turn for help!—would excommunicate Hitler before the damage was done. Thus, when the powerful man finally appeared and ceased to be that abstraction which their minds had been fond of conjuring, the intellectuals —and this is true for George and his followers too—perceived too late that the concretion was too brutal, too destructive, and too vulgar for their taste.

The other personality who, contemporaneously with Spengler, commanded the admiration of many young, sensitive, and intelligent Germans was the poet Stefan George. He, too, with his circle of intimates, confessed himself inspired by Nietzsche. However, he and his disciples read in Nietzsche a message which was not, like Spengler's, compressible into a simple formula of *Realpolitik*. In an essay on "Nietzsche as the Judge of Our Time," two members of the circle, E. Gundolf and K. Hildebrandt, claimed that it was they, the Georgians, who had actually begun to realize the new aristocracy of the mind for which Nietzsche had longed, and which was to give birth to a new German culture. Despite the general unpolitical accent which distinguished the Nietzsche worship of the George group, there issued from among them angry outbursts against democracy and humanitarianism occasionally matching the violence of Spengler. With a fierce tone in their voices, the Georgians would say that they would be glad if a "holy war" or a "holy pest" destroyed all such modernisms. They railed especially against the masses, which they called a "fiendish creation" of modern history, "the product of unbridled progress, lawless humanitarianism, and passive liberty." [11] But despite these mutual sympathies, Spengler looked upon the Georgians with contempt. To him they belonged exactly to those esthetes and literati whom he had pronounced historically impotent. He had, in his way, hit upon the chief difference. George was revered by his group as the Master precisely because he ignored the demands which the *Zeitgeist* had made with such insistence upon Spengler. It seemed to the Georgians that the creative power and the dignity of man were doomed to destruction unless it were possible for man to strike roots outside "modernity," outside its forces and conformities, its fads and vulgarities which degraded man to a mere social function and an appendage of apparatus. They believed that George had shown the way out of this corruption. His personality was to them the embodiment of classical nobility, and his poetry represented a heroic effort of preserving the purity and loftiness of the German language in the face of its appalling abuse to many low and mean intents.

Among the lesser lights of the group, those who did not know their own minds, hero worship took the forms of insipid and pious mystification of the Master and the snobbish consciousness of being exclusive. None perhaps remained wholly free of the milder affectations of idolatry. It is debatable whether the conscious solemnity and preciosity of George's work would ever have enabled it to carry the universal human message which his followers claimed for it. Gundolf, the most brilliant of their lot, realized the dangers of cliquishness and attempted to broaden the significance of the cult of the exceptional personality in which they were engaged. "Only one who respects what is higher than himself can also respect himself," Gundolf wrote.

The educational value of hero worship to a mind such as his was that it "increased our sense of responsibility, aroused our conscience, and moulded our character." The great man is one "whom one cannot love without acquiring a new measure of good and evil." [12]

This ideal of education, with which no humanist will quarrel, inspired the academic teaching, the literary work, and the scholarship of the Georgians. It gave the several historians in the group standards of selection and judgment so that there was no danger that, like so many an industrious but aimless scholar, they would be overwhelmed by the "material." Here and there in German universities the clarity of their aims was beginning to have a wholesome effect upon the uncritical positivism which had been the target of Nietzsche's satire. It was of course the biographies of great men to which their interests as historians were attracted, and having known the power of living greatness in their own lives, they were certain that such knowledge illumined their conception of greatness in the past. Thus Ernst Kantorowicz, at one time professor at the University of Frankfurt, wrote his great book on Emperor Frederick II. Gundolf, who taught in Heidelberg, produced studies of Caesar, Shakespeare, and Goethe, the last of which, a great success, offered a new type of literary criticism and interpretation. Ernst Bertram, professor at the University of Köln, in a biography of Nietzsche discharged the group's intellectual debt to the philosopher. None of these men respected the antiquarian notion of historiography. History here was a dialogue between the original and the re-creative mind, which ended in restoring the living reality of the one and in broadening the thought and sentiment of the other. These scholars agreed that their aim was to increase the interest in and respect for human individuality. This they did by attempting to show that great men, by their personality and their achievement, gave form to the times rather than being formed by them.

Of course this idea that history was the biography of great men had severe limitations. It had no use for either the Hegelian or the Marxian dialectics, and toward the latter the Georgians showed a pronounced hostility. In some cases, too, their scornful reaction against the type of scholarship which takes chief pride in pedantic drudgery reached the point of praising as a novel achievement the indulgence in a wholly subjective and fictionalized type of historiography. Bertram was an example of this extreme. He frankly termed his biography of Nietzsche (1918) "an attempt at a mythology" and in the Introduction to this work asserted that the essence of history evaded all rational means of knowing: the forms in which it most faithfully revealed itself were mythology and legendry, forms which developed in complete indifference to all available or procurable knowledge. Bertram further asserted that myths and legends were by no means an anachronistic form of tradition. He himself expected to restore it in this rational and skeptical age as the most genuine form of history. He claimed that it was the only history worth writing because it was the only one not fated to be forgotten. The task it assigned to the historian was a subjective, impressionistic portrayal of the images of great men as they appeared in the mirror of successive generations and ages.

In these assertions an echo of Nietzsche's theory of the superior value of monumental history was clearly audible. New, however, was the deliberate attempt to fabricate what supposedly were spontaneous myths with the elaborate help, it must be noted, of the modern press and library. This strange self-deception and intellectual dishonesty were resorted to by a mind which had obviously grown weary of the clear light of day and lost its power to endure a perfectly secular world. While freely interpretative writing has its place, Bertram seemed to have chosen this form partly because he wished to evade the rational criticism to which historical scholarship is always subject, partly also because this consciously "artistic" biography seemed to him a higher form of achievement than critical intelligence and industrious scholarship were capable of. He was the intellectual who had lost respect for himself and turned counterfeiter. All this happened, it is well to remember, without the slightest political compulsion. A critical intelligence, disarming and emasculating itself, initiated its own decadence. Perhaps Bertram did not, at the time, foresee the consequences. But in sanctioning what was little less than forgery, this university professor of more than local reputation helped to abolish the standards by which even the most patent falsification and historical quackery could be condemned. Thus when Alfred Rosenberg presented in *The Mythos of the Twentieth Century* (1930), the book which contains the Nazi version of the history of Western civilization, his brief had in principle already been furnished.

As everyone knows, the myths fabricated by Rosenberg were infinitely more ominous and potent than those of the George disciple, for they came to enjoy the backing of great political and military power. Any remaining scholars who were stubborn enough not to be mystified in the manner which Rosenberg desired were hard put to preserve their integrity. Their criticism came to be regarded as a profanity, if not a crime, against the National Socialist mythology. Bertram was not among those stubborn critics. He turned Nazi, which causes little astonishment, and became one of a number of German intellectuals who voluntarily undertook to defend National Socialism before the intelligentsia of the outside world. In a little volume entitled *Von der Freiheit des Wortes* (1934), he declared in a tone of noble indignation that the protests of the civilized world against the Nazi suppression of freedom in Germany were very ill advised. For, in contrast to certain other countries where the freedom of the word was shamefully abused, Germany, he said, held that freedom so sacred that her leading minds imposed upon themselves the dignity of silence.

There were others of the George group who turned Nazi, but the "circle" as a whole had no unified political opinion. Some of the members emigrated, and honestly detested Hitler and his order. Yet it is true that George and his disciples did less than prevent his coming. While their glorification of the imperial and noble personality was primarily an esthetic cult and the pastime of intellectuals, the cult was nevertheless associated with aristocratic social sentiments of a kind that cannot be pronounced politically innocent.[13] Their political romanticism confused rather than clarified the thinking of some of the best part of German academic youth in the critical years preceding Hitlerism. It also lacked the realism to foresee the inhuman conditions which a modern authoritarian government must create in order to maintain itself in power.

Spengler and George were the most serious but not the only leaders of anti-liberalism and anti-rationalism among German intellectuals. Outside their spheres of influence stood other personalities who reinforced these trends in a more esoteric way. Count Keyserling, for example, conducted a School of Wisdom at Darmstadt which attempted to introduce adult students to a philosophy combining oriental and occidental elements. Education in this school was distinguished by having no definite program or purpose of instruction. It was, according to Keyserling, living improvisation at the right moment and dealt exclusively with the "inspirational spring of life." The meetings of students were conducted by the Count according to the rules of "the art of spiritual orchestration." [14] To name another, Ludwig Klages, the graphologist, elaborated in his philosophic writings one of the favorite theses of irrationalism, the irreconcilable conflict and hostility between instinct and reason. He was later recognized by the Nazis as one of their philosophers. Rudolf Steiner, finally, organized an anthroposophic society. In a history of pre-Hitler irrationalism, these figures would deserve more detailed attention. But since none of them had direct relations with universities and their influence, if any, over university students was certainly small, they need not further occupy us here. They were too sectarian and, especially Keyserling and Steiner, too much the quack and charlatan to be taken seriously even by those who were impressed by Spengler or George.[15]

Of a very different caliber and more effective in helping to precipitate the crisis of the liberal university was the thought of three European writers and philosophers, Bergson, Tolstoy,

and Kierkegaard. Bergson's ideas about life as free and not mechanically determined, life as spontaneous vital impulse, and
intuition as the primary and most important mode of knowing,
were sympathetically received by a number of German philosophers. But on the whole his influence was too general to
be of great importance in this connection. Tolstoy was read in
Germany since the 1880's when the first translation of single
literary works of his appeared. His art does not concern us.
Relevant here are only some of his writings on science and
education which contain poignant passages on the despair of
the intellectual and the depreciation of scientific knowledge.
It was this phase of Tolstoy's thinking which, as one may see
from references in Max Weber, helped to provoke that critical
discussion of the meaning of *Wissenschaft* and its place in
higher education which engaged many leading German educators
and philosophers at the close of World War I. Most powerful and
most specific in its influence, however, was the philosophy of
Kierkegaard which inspired German existential philosophy as
well as modern Protestant theology. Kierkegaard's ideas, assimi-
lated and modified by such German professors as Martin
Heidegger and Karl Jaspers, entered into the minds of many
serious German students and reinforced, quite independent of
the influence of the men already discussed, the trend toward
anti-rationalism.

Kierkegaard, whose work began to appear in German translations in 1909, proclaimed the task of modern philosophy the
reverse of what it had been at its beginning in ancient Greece:
to turn indifferent to Platonic ideas and universals, and instead
gain insight into individual human existence.[16] To become a
self and to realize the uniqueness of individual existence, a
person must, according to Kierkegaard, become and then constantly remain conscious of his inner experiences. By these
Kierkegaard understood above all the radical and crucial decisions and risks in a man's life upon which he stakes the purpose and meaning of his existence. The more veracious and
abiding these decisions are, the greater will be the individual

person's sense of reality. That reality lies in the very sensitivity of his conscience which makes him aware of his terrible loneliness in the world, of his awful responsibility to himself, and of the inevitable sense of guilt should he fail himself. Kierkegaard's philosophy was founded in the experience of absolute religious despair, as was that of Augustine and Luther. Yet, at the same time, the ironical Socrates was to him the most congenial of all philosophers, and in Kierkegaard's own speech and writing irony and profundity lie strangely intertwined. Of chief importance in this connection, however, is Kierkegaard's definition of reality as a state of intense subjective inwardness, and as ethical and religious self-knowledge. Compared with this self-knowledge, knowledge of the external world as science, history, or even sociology was to him indifferent. In fact, Kierkegaard often remarked that the pursuits of knowledge, abstract or empirical, alienate the individual from his self and lead him into an anonymous world of generalization and convention. Such pursuits are only means of escape from the problems of existence. But since these cannot be escaped forever, the flight of abstract thought comes to a sad ending. The scientist and the system-building philosopher sink back exhausted into a life whose accidental nature they resent because it will not submit to predictions and systematization. There are in Kierkegaard, as in Nietzsche, ironical remarks about the "sad professorial figures" who busily cultivate their little plot and are forgetful of themselves and of the momentous, the terrifying, and the desperate. These, according to Kierkegaard, belong to the very essence of human existence. Like Nietzsche, Kierkegaard had a nineteenth-century sense of progressive dissolution and decay. But, unlike Nietzsche, he attempted to save himself by a restoration of the absolute truth of Christianity as if the modifying experiences of eighteen centuries could be forgotten.[17]

The effect which Kierkegaard had upon German academic philosophy was not altogether negative. He helped, like Nietzsche, to shock it out of an often arid preoccupation with technical and departmentalized questions, to restore to its inquiries a sense of urgency, and to broaden them so as to include the problems of human existence. Yet, the very manner in which Kierkegaard defined these problems again so narrowed German existential philosophy that its inquiries ended by isolating the individual hopelessly from society, from humanity, from history, or any rational community of spirits. This development, manifested in part by Karl Jaspers's *Geistige Situation der Zeit* (1931), reached its extreme with Martin Heidegger. Originally much indebted to the phenomenology of Edmund Husserl, Heidegger became, in the late 1920's and early 1930's, the most talked-about philosopher in Germany and attracted students from many parts of the world, including the United States. In his major work, *Sein und Zeit* (1926), Heidegger described human existence as prey to relentless anxiety and guilt, unredeemed by religious faith or even a sense of humility, a state from which man forever seeks to escape into the impersonal, unreal world of social convention, of gossipy joviality and *Das Man*, to try to find there at least a temporary relief from his desperate forlornness and his awareness of the certainty of death. But the two worlds of society and private existence, such as Heidegger described them, seem equally uninhabitable to a rational being. According to him, man has only the choice between a life which is unreal, hypocritical, and ingenuine, and a life which, spent in silent discourse with a guilty conscience, secures its authenticity from the ever-present sense that each must die his own death. One may ask, with Jean Wahl, whether "there is not a certain dignity in attaching to our death no greater importance than to that of another." [18]

This is however only a mild criticism. The chief objection to Heidegger's work is that in it the individual finds himself in a blind alley from which he can break out only by an act of blind faith and by surrendering, as Kierkegaard had already done, to some form of absolutism. The promised second volume of *Sein und Zeit* from which one could have expected the execution of this maneuver never appeared. The surrender on Heidegger's part, however, came just the same, only not to a religious but to a political dogma. In 1933, he turned National Socialist. I do not suggest that this act was a necessary consequence of *Existenz*-philosophy. While Heidegger collapsed, Jaspers, for example, did not. But the reason for this difference may have been that in Jaspers's philosophy human *Existenz* was not cast into absolute isolation from others. The conversion to Nazism seemed, in Heidegger, the fitting conclusion to a philosophy that described man as destitute of common loyalties and responsibilities, of humility and rational understanding. The destructive force of this philosophy is neither correctly nor adequately described by Aurel Kolnai when he says that its upshot is simply "never to let a moral consideration prevail against the command of your superior officer." [19] Such an oversimplification, and there are others in Kolnai's otherwise informative book, obscures the intellectual antecedents of Nazism. Without these, Nazism as merely the result of a temporary economic and political crisis would never have been taken so seriously in Germany. Without them, and without the various forms of irrationalism as here discussed, Germany would not have suffered in its educated class that confusion and moral paralysis which preceded the triumph of Nazism.

The writings in which Heidegger made his overtures to Nazism and in which, as teacher and rector of the University of Freiburg, he appealed to colleagues and students to follow his example, belong among the sorriest documents of that ignoble period. In his peculiar language, pretentious and profound in an obscure way, he proclaimed not only his own self-abasement but the degradation of philosophy in general to a lackey of the new state. Those "political" writings of his read like the testament of a thoroughly bewildered and bankrupt mind anxious to save itself at all cost. There is in Heidegger's declaration of allegiance to Adolf Hitler one phrase in which he himself seems to supply the reason for his action. "We have broken," he said with what seemed like an audible sigh of relief at having escaped the "nothingness" of his *Existenz*-philosophy, "with the idolatry of a bottomless and impotent thinking." The use of the first person singular here would have been more honest.[20]

Tolstoy, finally, helped to aggravate the crisis of rational thought by his simple thesis, which German irrationalism was predisposed to accept, that science is meaningless because it gives no answer to man's most important questions of how he should live and what he should believe. To Tolstoy, who had been aroused by the intensity and vastness of human injustices in a reactionary society, these questions were the only ones that mattered. In fact, they so preoccupied him in his later years that he became unappreciative of any art or science which did not directly aim at correcting social disorder and the resulting human degradations. Thus he impatiently demanded that science "must renounce its experimental method which causes it to consider as its duty the study of merely what exists and must return to the only reasonable and fruitful conception of science which is . . . to show how people ought to live." [21]

It was this doctrine of the meaninglessness of science, and the confusion of what is with what ought to be, which appealed to certain Germans and which more and more characterized the irrationalist revolt. The German irrationalists, however, had not the slightest sympathy with Tolstoy's humanitarian ideals. They were, as has been shown, social reactionaries and authoritarians with an occasional strain of sadism among them. Their revolt against science and reason, the revolution of *Wissenschaft* which had been impending since Langbehn, was singularly out of touch with, or openly hostile to, the social realities of the late nineteenth and early twentieth century. That is true for example of their attitude toward the ideas of Karl Marx and the labor movement, toward the Weimar republic and its problems, and toward modern technology in which even such a seemingly positivistic mind as Spengler saw at bottom a devilish creation.

Yet neither, as has been shown, did these irrationalists dwell firmly and freely in the kingdom of the mind. They were all latecomers to the criticism of modern civilization which more powerful minds, such as Kierkegaard and Nietzsche, had bequeathed to Europe. They labored under the impressions and diagnoses compellingly set forth by those men, who had so pre-judged the issues of the nineteenth and twentieth centuries that it was difficult for anybody to make a fresh analysis or gain a fresh aspect of them. Thus, doubly rootless, the irrationalists turned upon science and reproached it for its want of positive guidance and moral conviction, that is, of the very things which they themselves, as responsible and thinking men, should have provided. This spurious and idle reproach formed the substance of a turgid, confusedly written manifesto which, in 1920, pro-claimed that the time had come at last to establish a "new science." This was to be a union of empirical knowledge, speculative thought, and practical ethics. The little book, sig-nificant only as a document of the sterile intellectual excitement then prevailing in certain sections of educated Germans, came from the pen of a young George disciple and bore the title *Der Beruf der Wissenschaft,* or *The Vocation of Science.* This vocation, nebulously conceived of as some sort of mission, was defined in terms of service to the "higher needs" of the German nation. It was to be realized with the help of a new type of academic teacher who would no longer be merely scholar but leader and prophet, too.[22]

CHAPTER VI

THE LAST STAND OF RATIONALISM

ALL this confused romanticism, this demoralization of the mind by intellectuals afraid of the intellect, was a direct threat to the existence of the liberal university. It became urgent that the institution at last defend itself against the open charges and the insinuations which issued from those irrationalist and reactionary quarters. Merely to carry on, even successfully, its traditional activities and to hope that its record of professional competence and productivity would speak most eloquently for it, was no longer sufficient. To express once more one's faith in the "progress of science," or to deliver eulogies on scholarship of the kind claiming that the survival of culture depended upon the completion of a Greek dictionary, would indeed have carried no weight. The time for such naïvetés had passed. The questions which the university was now compelled to answer were crucial *educational* questions. Could the institution, at this critical juncture, still claim to educate a leading group of young people whose trust in reason was unshaken and who would demand the right to individual responsibility? Could the university prevent them from being seized by the infectious urge to surrender to fears and hatreds? Could it teach them, as it had never had to teach them before, how to control a complex civilization, not merely for the sake of efficiency, but so that they would remain human in the midst of a mechanical apparatus which tempts the destructive and the tyrannical in man? Could it inhibit that indulgence in an atavistic sense of guilt which, to some moderns, arises from the triumph of material achievements and once again seems to them to provoke the wrath of God? Could it, in short, help them to accept full responsibility for a world which has irrevocably become the product of the secular genius of man?

These were no simple questions for the defense to answer. A major difficulty was, and it still is, that such questions lie outside the scope of specialists who constitute the rank and file of university professors. Many were even unaware that such problems existed. What the defense wanted, then, was a distinguished scholar or scientist who could speak for the university as a whole and who also had a full grasp of the intellectual crisis inherited from the nineteenth century. For it was only from the broadest and deepest presence of mind that rationalism and liberalism might still summon strength for a last stand.

The man who had these qualities and who faced the task was Max Weber. A great sociologist and a scholar of extraordinary knowledge, Weber was a person of broad and varied interests which carried his inquiries far beyond any departmental specialism. He was conscientious and exact, yet without the pedantry and stuffiness of most academic men. He had too much vitality and his intelligence ranged too far to be confined within any academic "fields." He also wanted political responsibility— a record of his political actions and convictions is contained in a volume of *Politische Schriften*—and during the months immediately following the breakdown of the German Empire in 1918 and in the ensuing disorder, he worked for the emerging republic. If a lifelong nervous illness had not drained his strength, Weber might perhaps have played a political role in the Weimar Republic. Unfortunately he died at the age of only fifty-six, in 1920. A year before his death, the students of the University of Munich, to which he had recently come from Heidelberg, invited him to speak to them. The informal talk delivered on this occasion stands as an able and passionate defense of freedom, science, and reason.[1] It did not answer all the questions with which the liberal university was then besieged. Still it is in some respects one of the last great documents of German liberalism.

The year 1919 in Germany was a year of disorder. At Weimar, in the constitutional assembly, the future of the country was only just beginning to take form. In an atmosphere of uncertainty and insecurity German university students were asking themselves what their professional careers were likely to be, what social order and what political parties they should support, and where, in a period of revolutionary change and bitter political conflicts, they might find standards of judgment and truth. It was nothing less than Tolstoy's question about the meaning of life that concerned this post-war generation. What they wanted to know especially from their university teachers was whether and how *Wissenschaft* could illumine their search. Weber knew what was on their minds. He also knew that a distrust of rational thought was already abroad, a feeling which at any time might assume alarming proportions if nourished by a prolonged state of social unsettlement and insecurity. He therefore decided to impress upon his young audience from the outset the need for sanity and soberness of mind, and to caution them against any exaggerated expectation that the solution of the questions he proposed to answer would end all their difficulties.

He began by describing to them the work and career of a modern university professor in a manner which was free from illusions and pretensions, deliberately matter-of-fact and prosaic. What Fichte over a century ago, in his lectures to the students of Jena, had described with pathos as a divinely inspired mission, Weber now simply called a job, a job to be done as conscientiously as any other and without the invocation of absolutes. He made it clear that the development of modern science had long ago reached the phase in which its aims had become wholly secular and dissociated from the human quest for certainty and salvation. It limited itself now to the rational explanation and control of nature and society, and in order to realize these aims, scientific work moved from necessity toward constantly increasing specialization. Weber dwelt upon this point in order to dispel whatever false ideas concerning the glory of *Wissenschaft* his youthful audience might still secretly entertain. He warned that the only sort of original work anyone today could hope to do was a piece of highly specialized research. To accomplish it, scholar and scientist must put on blinders, as it were, and proceed as if the fate of the world depended upon the outcome of their work.

It may be noted at once that Weber, while advising his audience to rid themselves of illusions, at the same time required of the future young scientists an act of faith. Unless one assumes the existence of a cosmic order, which individual research may gradually help to illumine, such faith was either an act of great heroism, or it, too, was an illusion. One must further inject that the narrow and positivistic conception of science which he presented in his effort to sober young and confused minds, excluded as unscientific some of his own most original and fruitful work. In his inquiries into the methodology of the social sciences and in his studies of the relationship between religious ideals and economic systems, he himself had dropped those blinders. The result had been insights into problems which could not even have been brought into view by the one-track specialist. At times, therefore, Weber's words appear to be misleading and unnecessarily discouraging. At other moments, again, he succeeded better in making his meaning clear. This he did, for example, when he condemned the showmanship and charlatanism of certain professors who, having lost respect for solid work, attempted to make themselves "interesting," and to be "dramatic" to their students. That, Weber said, was like inviting the impresario onto the stage. Greatness in science as in art, he remarked, was achieved only by giving oneself completely to one's work.

From specialization Weber turned to a second characteristic of modern scientific work and to a second inevitability which, he knew, the students would find even more difficult to accept: that of all researches becoming obsolete in a relatively short time. For was not especially the young generation before him, uncertain of itself and its future, disposed to see in this a proof of the futility of a life devoted to science? The prospect of serving only as instruments for the increase of knowledge, the validity of which always remained provisional, was likely to repel them. Besides, with the catastrophe of World War I vivid in their minds, one could no longer expect them to make a religion out of the pursuit of instrumental knowledge. To demonstrate under these circumstances a more than utilitarian importance of *Wissenschaft*, to show that it was the inalienable property of the modern mind and a necessary element of its education was no slight task; but it was an essential one. One cannot say that Weber wholly succeeded in it. What actually he gave was an impassioned account, moving in its sincerity and absolute honesty, of the modern liberal's perplexity in a world of necessity. What he asked of the students was that they first of all face and learn to understand the problems and conflicts which, out of the intimacy of his own experience, he put before them.

His answer to the crucial question of the meaning of the unending pursuit of knowledge was that it is the instrument for the "rationalization" of the world. This "rationalization," by which Weber meant our desire and our ability to explain, organize, and control the forces of nature and the functioning of society, was especially important to Western man. It was in fact, according to Weber, the ultimate value, and from it *Wissenschaft* derived its value. In other words, Weber answered with a naturalist ethics, according to which good is what men desire, and is good because they desire it. But, being also a historical relativist, Weber knew that natural man was historically conditioned, and therefore he did not claim that the urge to rationalize the world was universal and everywhere equally developed. Only in Western rational philosophy, in Protestantism, science, technology, and bureaucratic organization had it found its greatest fulfillment, and here its importance grew the more man was forced to rely upon his creations for the very maintenance of civilization.

This historical naturalism could not, of course, convince those who no longer shared that basic Western urge and faith. There were those who, tired of that ceaseless "rationalization," felt

that Western genius was nearing its exhaustion for which precisely its own restive spirit was to blame. But Weber could remind them that, barring Western man's extinction, the problems
of the control of technics would remain with us, that human
freedom must be realized under the conditions which exist,
difficult as they may be, and that to expect its realization only
at the end of the machine age was to renounce it forever. What
at the moment Weber wished to bring home to his students
was not his belief in historical relativity—Scheler soon found
that here Weber was most vulnerable—but the secularization
of human morals. Here he was sound and he said what, in a
period of incipient pseudo-religiosity, needed to be said with
emphasis. It was, according to Weber, no longer possible for
a veracious mind to invoke divine or semidivine sanction for
the things it valued. To justify scientific pursuit by the belief
that it led to God, to a knowledge of substance, or to universal
progress and happiness—the latter having been the gods of
nineteenth-century scientific optimism—was characteristic only
of a few "overgrown children," some of whom still occupied
chairs in the universities. Weber implied that unless science was
separated from religion and morals, a confusion dangerous to
both would be prolonged. As in the case of the German
Darwinismus movement, science would become turgid, dogmatic,
and stagnant. Or, since no science could fulfill the moral and
religious hopes set upon it, it would end in disappointment and
disillusionment, thereby contributing to the rise of new religious
quackeries and to the revival of old dogmatisms. On the other
hand, man's moral responsibility was undermined if he entrusted
the realization of his ideals to some automatic process, such as
the progress of science is sometimes thought to be.

It was because of these dangers that Weber warned against
bringing "politics" into the classroom. The first principle of
teaching was to distinguish scrupulously between personal judgments of value and statements of fact. To abstain from the
first and to confine himself to the second was the discipline which
every teacher loyal to the spirit of *Wissenschaft* must impose

upon himself. Of course Weber, who was no Marxian, did not mean that historians and sociologists should exclude values from their study of the factors which are responsible for social change. But when so studied they should, he said, be treated as causes and stated as objectively verifiable facts. It was therefore an error on the part of students to demand from their academic teachers positive moral guidance and decisions, such as would be involved in answering the question as to what is the meaning of life. To attempt such an answer would transcend not only their work as scientists; it would also be a violation of the liberalism which Weber did his best to defend. Liberalism to him meant that the values for which life was worth living remained for the individual to decide, and it forbade the professor to relieve his students of this responsibility. Professors who politicized and moralized in their lectures were guilty of the worst abuse of academic freedom. In addition, Weber denounced them as political cowards and frauds. Not that he wished to defend those emasculated neutrals at whom Nietzsche had aimed his satire and who masked their lack of conviction and judgment as "objectivity." On the contrary, Weber deemed it everyone's *verdammte Pflicht und Schuldigkeit* to defend his own convictions, not, however, in the shelter of academic freedom and before audiences condemned to listen, but out in the open in political assemblies and in the press. There the plurality and the conflict of values were in daily evidence. There it was more difficult to be right, and everyone, even a German university professor if he dared enter the arena, was vulnerable.

To limit university teaching to rational and empirical knowledge did not, in Weber's eyes, condemn it to irrelevance or even meaninglessness, as Tolstoy and his German sympathizers had charged. Though the decision on life's ideals rested with the student, the university could help him see his ideal more clearly and instruct him in the knowledge necessary to realize it. Without such knowledge his decision was likely to be irresponsible and impractical. Then, too, Weber thought that the university could bring to the student's attention "uncomfortable facts" which would compel him to modify his beliefs. It could lead him to reflect on whether he could morally justify the means necessary for the realization of the end he desired, a question particularly relevant in a period teeming with revolutionary plans and ideas. Teaching of this kind obviously amounted to more than the imparting of information. It awakened the student's sense of intellectual responsibility and consistency.

In thus teaching young people the life of reason, Weber thought that he could go one step further. Without coming into conflict with science, and consistent with the principles of liberalism, the university could, in addition to intellectual training, assume a moral obligation. This consisted, according to Weber, in making the student aware of the conflict of moral world orders which always divide the loyalties of men. The mass of men either choose their values blindly and self-righteously, or, loath to make a decision at all since it entails a certain discipline of thought and action, remain indifferent, treating life as if it were a natural process. A liberal education could help at least some to choose their values knowingly, fully aware, as Weber put it, that in dedicating themselves to one god, they must thereby offend all other gods. He believed that man in our age could not attain maturity unless his mind was tempered by this philosophy of asperity and sober disillusionment. It was immature to despair at the inevitability of conflict and at the human inability to know absolute right. But it was senseless, too, to turn in alarm to *Wissenschaft* and to expect that it, like a superior court, could settle the strife with an "objective" verdict. To lament the meaninglessness of science when the error of such misplaced confidence finally becomes apparent, as it must, was to Weber simply the evidence of failing moral courage. That the modern liberal needed courage, Weber left no doubt. Pragmatist though he was, defending with William James the right of the individual to reach out for his own ideal of life, his pragmatism was not optimistic in temper and not wedded to the idea of progress. His was an ethics distinguished by the absence of illusions, an ethics of individual heroism necessary in a world in which conflict was permanent, certainty unattainable, communion with others rare, and life, in its essence, tragic. It was a pragmatism reminiscent of what Nietzsche, in *The Will to Power*, had called "the nihilism of strength": endurance to bear the destruction of all absolutes, with no sentimental turning back or rash embrace of new faiths, only the strength to hold out in the radical though bleak veracity of a cleansed mind. The task of helping the student achieve this veracity and maturity Weber assigned to philosophy in the university.

Weber's honesty, his directness and integrity were admirable. He concealed from his students nothing of the complexity of modern life and took them into his confidence, treating them as if they were already men and strong enough to withstand the cathartic he prescribed for them. Yet he erred pedagogically. It was improbable that youth could abide by a mere absence of illusions. Besides, the irrational and destructive forces, against which Weber wished to guard them, could be inhibited only by the vision of an ideal and a social ethos which once more would make possible that community for which people everywhere had already begun to long. But that vision Weber did not have. His thoughts reflected the end of an era.

As to the "rationalization" and secularization of the modern Western world, it is easy to see why they evoked in him no feelings of triumph. He described those developments without the glee which an old-fashioned atheist or iconoclast might have shown. He was merely concerned with making his students aware of a world in which it was more and more difficult to live without becoming dehumanized. He had observed, as a sociologist, the growth of bureaucracy in government and big business, as well as the division and increasing specialization of many forms of labor. The resulting atrophy of initiative, the avoidance of individual responsibility, and an overwhelming increase of purely functional intelligence caused him great anxiety. *Fachmenschen*, specialists of limited interest and little imagination who no longer shared a common world, were replacing men. Marx, who earlier was struck by the same menace of a wholly mechanical order of life, had summed up the human consequences in the term "self-alienation of man." But while both Marx's and Weber's diagnoses of this sickness of modern civilization were quite similar, their ideas of how to preserve the dignity of man differed radically. Weber, faithful to the spirit of bourgeois individualism even though he was critical of it, was unable to convince himself that communism could bring anything but a further bureaucratization of life. Already, he observed, society was full of people who became nervous and turned coward if the bureaucratic order ceased to function for a moment. "The question is," he said, ". . . what we may oppose to this machinery in order to preserve at least a part of man's life from . . . the autocracy of bureaucratic ideals of life." [2]

Weber's answer was that we must learn to live in two worlds at once: in the world of necessity as specialists, functionaries, and servants of a vast apparatus, and in the world of freedom as responsible and sensitive human beings capable of friendship and generosity. "It is the fate of our time . . . that the ultimate and sublimest values have withdrawn from public life, either into the outer-worldly realm of mysticism, or into the fellowship of direct individual relationships." [3] To his students he issued the warning not to mistake, in themselves or in others, the group man and *Fachmensch* for the full man. The dimension of humanity and the dimension of society were not identical. In fact, the dehumanization of man was assured by putting him wholly in bondage to the particular society in which he happened to live, and by estimating his worth, solely or predominantly, in terms of the function or service he performed in it. [4]

This general reflection leads back once more to Weber's definition of *Wissenschaft* which, too, is but one of those services or functions. Those who devote themselves to it are professionals and experts who produce and teach no more than instrumental knowledge. This, and not false modesty, was his reason for

saying, in the title of his address, that science was only an occupation (*Beruf*) like others, and that it was wrong to regard its
members as complete or superior men who knew better than
other mortals the answers to the problems of life. Weber felt
that, despite the criticism and satire by Nietzsche and others, the
academically certified intellectual continued in Germany to be
held in an esteem which, to his mind, was unfounded and un-
reasonable. At the end of his speech, he spoke out sharply against
the would-be leaders and prophets in academic chairs who,
sensing that something in the people was beginning to stir darkly,
tried to promote cults and movements. Weber was skeptical of
all prophets, and it saddened him that a people given the chance,
in 1919, to win some self-respect and rid itself of the heritage of
political docility, should demand any. Intellectuals, however,
trying to assume the role of prophet were to his mind plain
"swindlers." He was certain that they could never create a genuine community, but only an artificial cult or sectarianism.

Looking back over Weber's talk and the various strands of
thought woven into it, one has the impression of a man who was
extraordinarily sincere, sensitive, and alive, but also deeply troubled. The solutions he suggested for the problems of modern life
derived from an individualism which, though still militant, was
already oppressed by the thought that the values for which it
stood might be doomed to extinction. To some of the problems
discussed by him, other and more hopeful answers were possible.
To restrain the mechanization of modern life from growing even
more oppressive, more was necessary, it seems, than to retreat
into the intimacy of private life after one's work was done. But,
more important, the conflict between different moral orders
need not be as final as Weber made it out, if a deeper level of
experience could be reached on which human understanding and
communion could become more universal. To such an experience,
however, a university limiting education to the discipline of
science and to professional training gave no access. Weber possessed, as has been shown, a humanist sense of values, but
unfortunately his humanism remained *outside* the university. In

his conception of university training he neglected what is the essence of liberal education: the art of enhancing human understanding so that the individual may learn to free himself from his tragic isolation and come to feel himself a part of a common humanity. In this neglect lay perhaps the main insufficiency of Weber's ideas on university education.

Yet, in making this criticism, one must not forget his contribution. For those still willing to listen to rational discourse, Weber was the man of the hour who cleared the atmosphere of sultry romanticisms and who replied to that confusion of mind which tried to compound science and religion into a new and higher form of salvational knowledge. He showed convincingly how impossible it was to climb to heaven on the ladder of *Wissenschaft*. He also clarified, thereby, certain problems which under some of the earlier conceptions of higher education had not been fully solved, problems which concerned the relation of *Wissenschaft* and education. In the humanism of Wilhelm von Humboldt and in the idealism of Fichte, moral and educational imperatives had not been clearly distinguished from the aims of *Wissenschaft*, if the latter is defined as a system of empirical and rational knowledge. Knowledge of what is and of what ought to be, had in their thinking often flowed into one another. For Humboldt, for example, the study of classical antiquity, and, for Fichte, the study of idealist philosophy, had been the means of demonstrating to the student the validity of certain moral and educational values. It was upon this close relationship between ethics and science that, in the minds of those men, the educational importance of the university depended. Science for the mere sake of increasing our knowledge of the material world had not interested them, and the pursuit of science to this end would not, in their opinion, have qualified science as a fitting subject for university education.

Now Weber did not quarrel with the educational ideals of those men. He denied only that those, or any other, ideals grew out of, or could be proven valid by, the study of any branch of scientific knowledge. For in his opinion ideals were the spontaneous product of creative minds. Nor would he have denied that the educational ideals of the classical German period *inspired* academic study and teaching. In certain of his papers [5] he himself rejected the idea that scientists and scholars work without presuppositions. They obviously desire, he said, that their inquiries not only shall prove correct, but that they shall have significance. This presupposes interest on their part; it presupposes also a decision as to what is most worth knowing and this decision determines the choice of the problem and subject of the inquiry. Accordingly —and this is important because it shows how far Weber was from the positivism of which he was accused by Kahler—the questions which the scientist or scholar proposes to himself are not objective or scientific. At least they are unscientific in origin. They are the products of his imagination, his preferences and interests. Thus Weber, a great scientist himself, admitted that science depended for its human relevance and for its inspiration upon a life of the spirit. Yet at the same time he showed that once the inquiry was under way, it proceeded according to the standards of critical intelligence and scientific method, following an ideal of its own, which is to produce objective results in the sense that they may be verified by any other inquirer or observer. The truth of this is now so generally recognized that it may seem commonplace to repeat it here. But the fact is that these questions, which had been recurring for a century in discussions on the aims and nature of university education, were only now being clarified. Weber's position may be summed up by saying that he regarded as futile any attempts to establish the validity of an educational ideal upon scientific evidence.

One other thought in retrospect is here in order. Though it was true that the earlier idealist and humanist ideas on university study had lost most of their controlling influence, and that they contained a number of conflicts and tensions, it is also true that those ideas did not lose their challenge. The power to provoke thought and criticism must be recognized, despite the criticisms that have been made, as proof of the undeniable worth of those earlier educational philosophies. They were indispensable to creating that inner dialectic between ideas and realities which runs through the entire history of German educational thought as analyzed in these pages. This dialectic affords a central insight into that history; it accounts for the intellectual restlessness, the wealth and importance of the literature, and for the persistence with which the problem of a liberal university continued to be discussed in Germany. For that, there is no real parallel in other Western countries during the same period. Though the German university did in fact become more and more an institution devoted to scientific research and professional training, the idea that it *should be* an institution of liberal education was expressed by all its major critics, among whom were men deeply aware of the relation of education to human society.

With Weber the conflict between *Bildung* and *Wissenschaft*, liberal education and science, received clarification, but it was certainly not decided in favor of a liberal education. Weber put the emphasis upon what the university could *not* do. A convinced pluralist, he did not believe in the existence of a moral order, an order which might be said to exist wherever sensitive and intelligent persons exist through whose common understanding this order is enhanced. Accordingly, university teaching, as he saw it, could make people agree only on causal relations; it was dominated by the mode of thought characteristic only of science. The more important, and certainly the more difficult part of a liberal education, that of teaching young people to perceive in their relations with each other the existence of certain common values without which a community cannot exist, was the problem which he left untouched.

This, however, was precisely the problem on whose solution the success of the democratic reorganization of the German society initiated in 1919 in part depended. Among the educationists and philosophers of the Weimar Republic who were concerned with this problem, there was only one, Max Scheler, who succeeded in transcending Weber's relativism and who emerged with a radical and comprehensive plan for the reform of German higher education. Before proceeding to the analysis of Scheler's ideas, it is necessary to review briefly the economic and political conditions of the 1920's in so far as they are relevant to his plan.

The difficulties which, from its inception, beset the Weimar Republic proved greater than Weber had foreseen. The pressures of political parties growing in radicalness; the emergence of movements with murky ideologies; economic insecurity and widespread impoverishment, resentment, and conspiracy among the upper and middle classes against the Republic; disaffection in the very ranks of its officialdom—those were the social realities in which that post-war generation of students grew up, to whose integrity of reason Weber had appealed. Even if a majority of professors continued to teach the life of reason, it was inevitable that the university as a whole should be affected by the insecurities and anxieties of the mass of students who began to flock to the institution in alarming numbers. They were driven not by any passion of the intellect, but by the attempt to save themselves from economic destruction in the lower levels of the social structure from which, for the most part, they came. The illusion of climbing to safety on academic "privileges" lodged itself in their minds.

It is impossible here to go fully into the sociology of German higher education. Only the conditions most adverse to liberal culture and education may be briefly touched upon. In the first place, certain inroads upon academic freedom were made under the Republic which here, as in many other instances, was too weak in resisting the power of certain political parties and too willing to make them concessions to insure their "co-operation" in other matters. Thus, at several universities, chairs for "Marxist science" and, in appeasement of the opposite clerical party, chairs for "Catholic philosophy," were established. Both were contradictions in terms, since Marxism is not a science and Neo-Thomism is a philosophy inseparable from Catholic dogma. The teaching of class and church dogma was a violation of the principles of liberal teaching. Apart from this, however, academic freedom suffered no further important infringements.

A second threat, already mentioned, was the rapid and unsound increase in student enrollments in the universities and in all other institutions of higher professional training. As the educational-sociological literature of that period in Germany indicates, this was a central problem in higher education. The increase was heaviest between the years 1925 and 1930, but its fatal effects did not become visible until the early thirties when, in the depths of the depression, students of dentistry, medicine, engineering, and secondary education—this was the order in which the professions were most affected—had completed their training only to find themselves among the growing ranks of an "academic proletariat," embittered and disillusioned. That the universities were overcrowded may be measured also by the fact that in 1933 the number of students graduated from all institutions of higher learning was nearly double the number the national economy was able to absorb in positions for which the students had prepared.[6]

In addition to this lack of educational planning, there was a third factor which spoke particularly ill of the new democracy: only 5.8 per cent of all students at German universities in 1930 came from the ranks of industrial and agricultural labor. The upper middle class (ranking officials, army officers, professional men, industrial owners and managers, and big landholders) supplied 31.7 per cent, while the considerable majority, 60.7 per cent, came from the lower middle class (subaltern officials, clerks, elementary-school teachers, small shopkeepers, and farmers).[7] This meant that the university and with it the secondary school remained, in fact, middle-class strongholds. But for the most part it was a middle class which, impoverished and unnerved by the 1923 inflation, made desperate efforts not to sink down into the mass of proletarian workers.

Both teaching and learning suffered directly from over-crowding. It was common to have hundreds of students attend lectures in the larger universities, such as Berlin, Munich, Leipzig, and Cologne. Seminars often had over fifty students, which made individual participation in discussion nearly impossible. Personal contact between teacher and students, except for the gifted few who attracted the teacher's attention, was impossible. Most students worked harder than was customary before 1918, and they were more conscientious in their attendance at lectures, but were forced to curtail their studies to the very minimum of courses required to pass the final examinations. Only a few still enjoyed the leisure to read and audit courses outside their professional studies.

It would be a gross injustice to the loyal and courageous friends of democracy in Germany, in the education ministries of the states as well as in local communities, in the adult education movement, and in the universities, to assert that they did nothing to cope with these critical problems. A number of minor reforms and innovations were actually introduced in the universities,[*] and a considerable literature in the 1920's testifies to the concern which the future of the institution aroused not only in academic but in government circles as well. Yet it is also true that from the members of these circles, with the single exception of Scheler, no radical reform plan emerged. Whether such a plan, which would have had to include the entire system down to the *Volksschule*, did exist and whether it was suppressed from fear of offending this or that party with which the government found itself compelled to bargain, only those then in responsible positions can say. The fact is that in the discussions of the future of higher education in the twenties and even in the early thirties, traditionalist thinking prevailed.

Evidence for this may be found in its best form in the ideas and in the work of Carl Heinrich Becker, the most outstanding minister of education (1925–1930) in Prussia during the Weimar period. Becker, a humane man and a great Islam scholar, was historical-minded, loyal, and even reverent toward German academic traditions and values which he hoped to preserve in a period of stress and social change. He introduced, it is true, several educational reforms. But with regard to the university, his admiration for the early nineteenth-century ideals was so great that he hoped once more to revive the unity of *Wissenschaft* by bringing together in a single organization, namely, the university, all branches of learning, including even the separate institutes of higher technical and professional education. Becker once referred to the universities as *Gralsburgen der Wissenschaft*, a noble appellation suggesting seclusion and retreat where men might devote themselves undisturbed to research and philosophical reflection. Unfortunately the period after 1919 made it impossible for most students, and for many professors too, to dwell in that ideal sanctuary. Becker seems to have thought that the values of reason and science could best be preserved by isolating the university from the adverse social conditions of the time. This anxiousness to preserve, rather than the courage to reinterpret and re-enact, the values of a liberal education, even if this should require new methods and institutions, was characteristic of most of the leading German educationists of that time.

The single great exception, as I have said, was Max Scheler. In his later years Scheler's restive and searching mind turned from philosophy to sociology, and in 1926 he published what is probably his most important work on the sociology of knowledge and education, entitled *Die Wissensformen und die Gesellschaft*. In the pursuit of these inquiries he acquired a knowledge and showed a grasp of the relation between education and society which the old-fashioned liberal lacked. Scheler also had a religious bent which added to his knowledge a passionate concern for the spiritual welfare of man in modern society. There was in him a longing for a new community which would transcend Weber's individualism of lonely souls, private gods, and purely intimate personal values, a longing to bring people together by more than economic interest and activity.[9] The aim which inspired his last writings—Scheler died at the age of fifty-four in 1928, just when men of his kind were desperately needed in Germany—was the realization of a "social humanism," to borrow a term from Thomas Mann, and to this task he brought not only the necessary faith in man, but a radical thought and a well-outlined plan for the reorganization of German education. The very existence of a man of Scheler's moral resources proves that

Germany at that time still possessed recuperative powers which deny Spengler's doctrine of the country's spiritual exhaustion. Scheler was too creative a thinker to accept either fascism or communism as the only alternatives to a bankrupt economic liberalism. Dissatisfied with the latter, and dreading the former alternatives, he projected a system of education which sought to reconcile freedom with order, and social change with a humanist sense of values. This plan remained on paper during the Weimar Republic, and, of course, it was never heard of under the Nazis. It is possible, however, that if and when the time arrives for the rebuilding of Germany, some of Scheler's ideas may yet come to fruition.

Scheler's central criticism of the German academic tradition was that the university had assumed more responsibilities than any one institution could possibly discharge. At one and the same time it tried to provide opportunities for professional training, scientific research, and liberal education, three types of pursuit which, in his opinion, were incongruous and in part mutually conflicting. He differed radically from Becker in that he rejected the older conception of the *universitas* of knowledge, because it seemed to him to have imposed upon the university a primitive form of organization inhibiting the growing differentiation of its three interests. He recommended, therefore, that the reform of German higher education begin by dividing the three pursuits among three distinct institutions, one devoting itself to professional training, another to scientific research and a third to that which had been most neglected, liberal education.

Under this plan the existing university was to be transformed into what in fact it already was, though with a "bad conscience," namely, an aggregate of professional schools, but relieved of the duties of both research and liberal education. The advantages which Scheler expected to accrue from this were several. A greater efficiency and thoroughness in professional training would be achieved by reorganizing courses to this end and by entrusting them to experienced practitioners of law, medicine, and so on. As things stood, the professors who taught the large required professional courses regarded themselves principally as scholars or research men, and accordingly treated their teaching duties perfunctorily. The result was that more often than not teaching was dull and badly organized, so that students resorted before the final examinations to the cramming schools which were abundant in every German university town. Apart from this inefficiency, Scheler regretted that students under the existing system seldom received any ethical counsel or guidance before entering practical professional work, because the traditional professor in Germany scorned such "practical" problems. Teachers for secondary schools, trained at the universities, acquired quite often a wealth of information and sometimes scholarly ambitions or pretensions. But they did not learn how to win the respect and confidence of their students, or how to teach. Under his plan, professional education was to give more attention to these matters.

In proposing, second, separate institutions for research, Scheler's argument was that scientific inquiry and utilitarian-professional work follow different lines of interest. Under the existing organization, problems which did not fall clearly within the province of any recognized academic discipline were often neglected. In other words, in an institution dominated by professional interests, inquiry was not really free. It could become so, he suggested, only in institutes which would carry on their work independently, though they might remain affiliated with universities. "The objective relations of matters into which the scientist inquires lead the mind along lines very different from those prescribed by the functional organization of knowledge." [10]

Most important to Scheler himself was the third part of his plan which sought to establish separate educational colleges. The education of man, which Scheler conceived in terms other than a merely pragmatic conception of life, was the most neglected of all academic responsibilities. With this certain of his contemporaries, for example Eduard Spranger, agreed. But they thought that the universities might yet save liberal education by simply giving greater prominence to the philosophy of the various subjects taught. Scheler remained unconvinced by this argument. As long as the traditional scholar or research-man did the teaching, philosophical reflection and criticism would continue to receive inadequate attention simply because it seemed to that type of teacher "unproductive" or even a waste of time. Scheler proposed, therefore, separate educational colleges for which the *Collège de France* seemed to him to offer a certain model.

Scheler planned the education in these colleges in one sense as a weapon against the mental inertia of professional routine and against the student's piddling immersion in accidental facts. The student was to be given broad syntheses of knowledge in order to let him see the matrix of conceptions and hypotheses in which all empirical knowledge lies ordered and embedded. Scheler spoke of the Platonic idea, not as an entity in itself but as the ability, developed through education, of seeing the universal in the particular. To his mind, this was always one of the distinctions of an educated man, but not necessarily of the scientist or scholar. Scheler of course did not deny that education makes use of the knowledge supplied by science and scholarship. But education is distinguished from these by the individual effort, which each mind must make, of creating out of that knowledge an ideal, or ideational, structure of reality. In this sense, philosophy was an indispensable part of a liberal education. The highest purpose of both philosophy and education was not to teach the individual how to predict or control the course of events, but to learn to know himself as part of an objective order which, Scheler said, man does not change or control, but which he may understand and thereby enhance. Such understanding Scheler, in similarity to Spinoza, described at times as intellectual love or cosmic sympathy. He always thought of it, lest there be any doubt, as a form of knowledge no less rational than, though distinct from and superior to, the pragmatic knowledge which he assigned to the professional schools. To repeat, Scheler was convinced that man could become fully human and rational only by transcending the pragmatic conception of life. He used the term *Bildungswissen* for the type of knowledge by which man, with the help of great literature, entered into communion with other minds and, thus humanized, learned to perceive the existence of a common moral order. The metaphysical or speculative by which man learned to project a rationally possible cosmic order, he termed *Erlösungswissen*.[11]

At this point the differences between Scheler and Weber become especially apparent. Weber could not logically have suggested educational colleges of the sort proposed by Scheler because there would, in fact, have been nothing for them to teach. *Wissenschaft* to Weber meant the advancement of instrumental knowledge and nothing more. It was to him the only knowledge capable of objective rational statement and, therefore, of being taught. In Scheler's mind, *Wissenschaft* assumed again a more inclusive meaning. Not that he had any more sympathy than Weber with what he called "feeble-minded romanticism." He believed, however, that not only the material world which concerns our pragmatic intelligence, but also the moral and the religious life of man contain elements of universal agreement which could be further developed and strengthened in the minds of the students through rational and undogmatic teaching. He planned his educational colleges with this end in view, thus trusting reason and its formative power farther than Weber had. The latter, it is true, had thought it necessary to acquaint students with the variety of ethical systems. But since he believed morals to be a matter of taste, that is, of subjective, irrational choice, the students chose, in fact, in the dark. Philosophy might in that case be merely a means for rationalizing one's faith. Now Scheler did not deny the reality of moral conflicts, but it did not oppress him with the same tragic finality. Unlike Weber he did not believe in the equal validity of all moral claims but thought that there existed criteria by which to sift them out. Speaking once of the future of Europe, Scheler said that the continent had arrived at a point in its history where it simply could no longer afford to indulge and humor just any ethics or political ideology. Absurd national vanities, ambitions, and murky sentimentalities were certain to hasten the destruction of European civilization. Thus in one of the several appeals he made for the establishment of a European university, Scheler said that the first duty of the institution must be to make the youth of all European nations aware of the *common* culture and ideals of the continent, of the *common* dangers threatening it, and also of the *common* contribution which Europe, in contrast to America and the Orient, had to make to world civilization.[12] This is an illustration of how Scheler hoped to demonstrate and teach the existence of a certain order in the world of values no less than in the world of material things.

It is important to realize that Scheler, in going beyond Weber, nowhere succumbed to the temptation of dogmatic teaching, but remained faithful to the spirit of the liberal university. This becomes particularly clear from what he had to say about the teaching of metaphysics in the proposed colleges, a subject which today arouses in many minds suspicions of absolutism. Scheler did not favor any one system of metaphysics. Nor was religious certainty the value with which he was here primarily concerned. Having gone through a brief period of sympathy with the Catholic Church, he had come to realize, "gradually and painfully" as he said, his error of supposing that Thomism was separable from church dogma. Later, in his sociological writings, he described how dogmatic theology had in fact always been the inveterate enemy of free metaphysical thought, and how the development of metaphysics had been inhibited also by modern positivism. To Comte, for instance, philosophical speculation had been a more primitive interest than scientific inquiry, in whose favor, he predicted, philosophy would be abandoned. For Scheler, who attacked Comte's positivism,[13] metaphysics was, on the contrary, a permanent and growing interest of the human mind, and one that could not be frozen into the Thomistic-Aristotelian or any other system. He took issue with those who argued that "it was impossible for man to endure an unfinished god," in other words, to believe in a cosmic order which might be said to grow wherever courageous and imaginative minds were at work. Metaphysics, according to him, was never "an insurance for weak, dependent men," [14] but the supreme adventure of which the rational mind was capable. Yet, by demanding for his colleges complete *libertas philosophandi*, he had no intention of humoring individual arbitrariness. If speculative thought was to result in enlarging human understanding of the cosmic order, it must impose upon itself a threefold discipline. It must, in developing "probable hypotheses concerning the ultimate structure of things," have "reference to the current state of scientific knowledge." [15] It must, secondly, have absorbed the most important insights of preceding thinkers; and, thirdly, it must proceed from as comprehensive an experience of the present state of the world as is possible for an individual thinker. Speculative thought, since it does not start from wholly demonstrable premises, obviously cannot be proven either true or false. Yet a certain measure of validity for a metaphysical hypothesis may be found, according to Scheler, in the fact of its being accepted by other thinking men because their own experiences suggest it as probable and meaningful. Thus the value of philosophical speculation to young minds was that it stimulated them to follow ideas attempting an imaginative completion of the world in which we live; that through such ideas they joined in the aspirations of others like them; and, finally, that speculative thought demanded the greatest integration of individual thought and experience. Scheler frequently stressed the fact that philosophy so understood was always the achievement of a single individual, never the result of a co-operative division of labor as in science. This was another important reason why he thought philosophy a more humanistic discipline than scientific research.

It is unnecessary here to go into the details of the organization and operation of the educational colleges. Many questions were left open by Scheler himself, and only the following points may be briefly touched upon. The colleges, in distinction from the universities, were to be free from state control and supervision. The reason was, according to Scheler, that a humanist education transcends the narrow interests of the state in education. In these colleges the individual student, released from the pressure and strain of his professional preparation and from nationalist fetters of his mind, should gain access to the world of cosmopolitan thought. All university students, preferably after completion of their professional and technical training, would attend a number of basic courses in the humanities. Professional men already established in their practice would return periodically as students in order, as Scheler put it, to keep their minds active and alert upon a high level of European culture. The administration of the colleges would remain decentralized, and the local intelligentsia would have a voice in the selection of the teaching staff. Teachers were to be chosen for their intellectual vigor and synoptic power; and to a far greater extent than the ordinary university professor had ever been, they were to be examples of moral personalities formed by independent and responsible thought.

There remains one important part of Scheler's plan, and that is the establishment of *Volkshochschulen*, or adult education centers, as part of a reorganized system of higher education. Scheler realized that democracy, in order to survive in Germany, needed a broader basis of common values than an unfortunate political and social history had left her. He also realized that Germany still lacked sufficient leadership by men of intelligence, ability, and character, without which democracy was likely to be manipulated by mercenary interests. The *Volkshochschulen* were to help recruit leadership from the working classes whose constructive powers had hardly been tapped and for whom the schools were primarily intended. Scheler made it clear that he wished to dissociate these schools completely from the older university extension movement. Higher education for the people needed a far more vigorous support than the universities had given, or could give, occupied as they were with their own specific interests. It was even more important to free adult education from the aura of charity which had surrounded it, and to allay the workers' suspicion that the bourgeoisie, entrenched in the universities, was using adult education as a means to appease them and to counteract Marxism. It was one of Scheler's aims to eliminate, through these schools, the hostility which existed between bourgeoisie and proletariat. He wanted to awaken in working men sympathies that went beyond class solidarity, beyond the struggle for political power and material betterment. He hoped to enhance their capacity for a broader human solidarity. In these hopes Scheler was encouraged, he said, by intelligent workmen themselves who had begun to recognize the human barrenness as well as the economic errors of orthodox Marxism, an awakening which may have come in part as a consequence of the costly failures of the Comintern in Germany in the 1920's.[16]

The educational program of these *Volkshochschulen*, which Scheler hoped to see established in all major cities, closely resembled that of the colleges. But since these schools were primarily intended for working class people, teachers were to take special care not to obstruct their work by technical and academic jargons. Scheler realized that to reach the mind of the common man with ideas and values that had generally been regarded as beyond his interest and understanding was a new and difficult venture in teaching. Its solution required more than a new technique. It required a social ethos and a faith, to use a word of the good Pestalozzi, *in die vergrabenen Kräfte des niederen Volkes*. It also supposed some form of living contact with the modern industrial worker and his problems. For these reasons Scheler did not wish the teaching staff, except for an initial period, to be selected from the ranks of university professors. Equally undesirable were young academic instructors without practical knowledge who, seeking only to supplement their incomes or to experiment with their teaching, would compromise the schools. Propagandists and cheap popularizers also had to be kept out. The best way to create a staff for the task at hand and to maintain high standards seemed to Scheler to train it in the universities where he advised the establishment of special institutes and professorships for "social pedagogics." [17] In addition to training teachers for adult schools, these institutes would open opportunities for research in a field of work which, Scheler believed, no nation interested in more than the material welfare of its people could longer afford to neglect.

The great responsibility of adult education at a time when the German people were trying to understand and to accustom themselves to a democratic order was evident. Scheler hoped that these schools would conduct in a rational spirit discussions of many national and international problems, and that they would help clear away resentment and fears, ignorance and long-standing prejudices. Among the foremost evils which they should seek to eliminate, he mentioned the old strife between Catholics and Protestants in Germany, the "feeble-minded" modern romanticism and irrationalism, the growth of irresponsible fascist movements, and the class hatred fomented by reactionary bourgeoisie and orthodox Marxism alike. Though Scheler meant these schools to provide a general education in the arts and sciences, their work was to have special relevance to these larger problems of the present. The test of the quality of a general education was, he repeated, that the student learn to recognize problems of universal human significance in the particular shape which they assumed under existing conditions, thereby becoming better capable of making responsible decisions concerning them.

It should be noted that whenever Scheler spoke of social education with regard to these schools, he thought of it as something far more difficult than making people "socially responsive." The latter words frequently occur in pretentious educational writing in America today. But if mere responsiveness were the criterion, National Socialism for example would have qualified as a social education. Scheler's point was that social education must not be separated from liberal education. Separation would bring an amoral behaviorism, and teachers could do no more than establish a hollow fraternity on the basis of social conformity. He was opposed also to popularizations and over-simplifications of knowledge and thought. Democracy did not mean for him a leveling of intelligence and imagination. Instead of "bringing education to the people," the adult schools would have the difficult task of selecting from among the workers an elite whom they would introduce to values, upon the understanding and renewal of which depended the survival of German and European culture. The adult schools were to broaden the sense of human solidarity, not only as this is required by modern co-operative economic enterprise, but for imaginative discourse between free and responsible men.

It is not surprising, therefore, that Scheler did not wish to burden these schools with vocational education. He may have thought that Germany already possessed better vocational training than most countries, a training which was based on old traditions of craftsmanship and which supplied the nation adequately with competent and skilled labor. What was needed, as other critics of German higher education had also stated, was a responsible rather than a functional intelligence. But Scheler, in his plan of adult schools, was the first to attack this problem systematically and realistically. He was as convinced as Max Weber that the labor of the modern industrial worker had been narrowed and mechanized to a degree where it could no longer be made the basis of an adult education. This is a view contrary to John Dewey's, who believes that the occupations should be the basis of a "continuous education," and that this education should attempt to broaden the meaning of practical work by associating with it scientific and social interests. With this Scheler disagreed. He thought that the only means of rescuing the worker's humanity was for the adult schools to take him completely out of his sphere of daily work in order to make him aware that there are other than mechanistic and pragmatic modes of thought. The root of the difference between Dewey and Scheler lies in their conceptions of what constitutes a liberal education. This is not the place for a full comparison of the views of the two philosophers. But since Dewey has shown an interest in the deficiencies and in the final catastrophe of German culture and has, in fact, offered an explanation of his own, his views are here of interest and may, in conclusion, be critically reviewed.

Dewey believes, contrary to Scheler, that the chief aim of liberal education in a modern democracy is to make men aware of the scientific basis of industrial processes and, in general, to teach people to assume an experimental attitude toward the problems of life. Dewey gives the impression of being afraid of ideals. They seem to him for the most part abstract and fixed, empty yet at the same time capable of exacting from men some form of blind obedience. He finds this fear abundantly justified when he looks at the course of German philosophy and politics since Kant.[18] German philosophy, in Kant even more than in Fichte and Hegel, appears to him to have produced a series of abstractions and absolute ideas which, far from being innocuous playthings of the intellect, have come to serve as a cloak and justification for political absolutism and fanaticism. Kant, whom Dewey considers guiltier than the others, epitomized this dangerous abstractness in his categorical imperative which to Dewey is nothing but an empty, formal concept of duty. Dewey points out, however, that its extreme formality allowed certain German nationalists of the nineteenth century to give it a very specific content which, as he shows with quotations from Bernhardi, helped to promote German aggressiveness and militarism. He concludes from this evidence that fine sounding ideals can do, and in the case of Germany have done, irreparable harm: in fact Kant's categorical imperative, he says, merely "calls up the drill sergeant." [19] Dewey goes so far as to say that the idealism of Kant, Fichte, and Hegel, whom he calls the "educators" of the German people, has made the people receptive to Hitler and *his* idealism. Between those idealists and Hitler is a "strand of continuity." For just as Kant sharply divided the world of necessity from the world of freedom, subordinating the first to the second, so Hitler, "along with the glorification of force expressly states its subordination (military and economic alike) to ideas and ideals." [20] In Hitler's success, therefore, Dewey sees "a tragic warning of the danger that attends belief in abstract absolute 'ideals.' " [21]

Dewey is correct in his criticism of the emotional cloudiness and the abstractness of much of German Idealist philosophy. He is also correct in saying that the mere affirmation of ideals is not enough, and he justly finds in Germany much lack of intelligent discussion of what ideals mean in human experience and in concrete social situations. Yet it is surprising that he should hold Kant chiefly responsible. When Dewey says that Kant's concept of duty merely evokes the picture of military obedience, he agrees with the interpretation which certain German nationalists have given to that concept. But this interpretation is not necessarily a valid one. It is, in fact, refuted by Kant himself, who says that the moral imperative is binding upon all who regard man as rational, free, and responsible; that it forbids us, if we claim these attributes, to use another person as means to our selfish ends. In the *Foundation of the Metaphysics of Morals*, Kant has illustrated the meaning of this moral law. He says there that it does not allow us to lie, to enter into contracts only to break them later when it is to our advantage to do so, to suppress the free development of other men's powers, or to remain indifferent to the sufferings of others. For if we so acted, Kant proves, we would destroy the moral order without which a common humanity cannot exist. One can hardly call this idea of morality empty and formal. Dewey would certainly agree with Kant in this, that anyone who denies the freedom of others, thereby destroys his own. Thus Dewey's judgment of Kant is difficult to understand, except that it may be a protest against the form of Kant's reasoning which is *a priori* and deductive throughout.

My own conclusions, formed in this study, do not concur with Dewey's explanation of the catastrophe of German education and culture. "Germany," so Dewey wrote recently, "in particular has been the home of the practices and the philosophy based on strict separation between science as technical and ever changing and morals conceived in terms of fixed, unchanging principles." [22] Dewey is correct if he refers here to the German inclination to obey any form of state authority. [23] However, taken as a general explanation, the statement obscures rather than

THE LAST STAND OF RATIONALISM

illumines the problem. Dewey practically ignores the destructive power of the anti-rational and illiberal philosophies analyzed in the previous chapter. He maintains, for example, that Hitler had less use for Spengler than perhaps for any other German philosopher, and that it was Kant and Kantianism, which he calls the "orthodox" German philosophy, that first cast the German mind into its fatal mold. It seems a tortured interpretation of history to establish continuity between Kant and Hitler while passing over the irrationalists and the contempt for peace and humanitarianism which unite Spengler, despite his pessimism, with Hitler.

Finally, it is not a valid objection against a moral law to say that it is stated abstractly; so are scientific truths. The meaning of either does not become clear until a general truth is applied to particular situations, and in either case, too, dogmatic and unintelligent teaching is possible and fairly common. The task of liberal education is precisely to help young people translate abstractions into concrete meanings, and to throw old ideas into fresh combinations. It is true of course that social conditions change. But the conclusion to be drawn from this fact is not that the educator's attention should be exclusively riveted to the instruments by which to effect that change. He must not neglect the moral ideas which, abstractly as they may be stated, contain a fund of human experience. This fund will be diminished and dissipated, however, unless the meaning of those ideas is reinterpreted and re-enacted by us who live among those changed conditions. Or else their meaning will indeed be lost and vitiated in the manner described by Dewey. When liberal teaching so succeeds in reinterpreting an old truth, it does far more than make us re-think and reiterate the ideas of the great, although this is the accusation usually brought against those who insist upon the use of great literature in education. It actually *enlarges* the meaning of those ideas. Kant's moral philosophy, for instance, was written before science and technology transformed the conditions of modern life. This fact, though it does not invalidate his philosophy, makes it necessary to reinterpret it in the light of those conditions. To put it differently, students who bring to the reading of Kant a knowledge of modern society and its problems are likely to find him "creative reading": he will be for them a profitable exercise in suggestive and imaginative thinking. His idea that man is an end in himself has in various forms and varying degrees been violated and denied by capitalism, fascism, and communist dictatorship. Each of these systems of society imperils in its own way the existence of a common humanity. But Kant, together with other thinkers of the past, may help us to reflect upon ourselves and to discover the common root of these perils. How they may be met effectively neither he nor the instrumentalist of the present is alone able to say. Education which aims at imaginative thought requires the services of both. To have ignored this rather simple truth explains, it seems to me, the heated but sterile controversies of past versus present, of science versus humanities, and of liberal versus vocational education, which constitute so large a part of contemporary American philosophy of education. The fact that Scheler, despite the fragmentary quality of his work, not only avoided these alternatives but suggested how ideas may be infused into realities, gives his educational philosophy a greater than historical significance. Perhaps these pages may help those who have begun to work for the educational reconstruction of Germany to rediscover it.

EPILOGUE

In the years following Scheler's death in 1928 the radicalization of the German masses proceeded rapidly under aggravated economic conditions. In the absence of inspiring and courageous democratic leadership, a sense of approaching crisis and disaster began to affect men's thoughts and action. Many believed that the country was drifting into a state in which its most pressing social problems could be solved only by extreme measures of either the political right or left. The universities were unable to remain islands on which the unpolitical scholar and scientist could live in seclusion from the fierce agitation mounting on all sides. Not only were students disturbed by the uncertainty of future employment and inevitably concerned with political issues; but already, years before Hitler was made chancellor, groups of nationalist conspirators and, later, Nazi students began to foment unrest and provoke violence inside the universities. The cases of Professor Gumbel at Heidelberg as early as 1925 and Professor Dehn at Halle in 1931 are among the best known of those early incidents: both men were publicly insulted and threatened for their anti-nationalistic convictions by groups of rowdies who finally succeeded in intimidating and confusing even the faculties.

The universities, then, had ample and direct warning. There was time to prepare for militant resistance against political violations of academic freedom. The customary meetings of academic societies were occasions at which declarations of the solidarity of intellectuals might have been drawn up and a general alarm given. The annual conference of the Association of the German Universities *(Deutscher Hochschulverband)*, especially, could have issued a manifesto tantamount to an expression of non-confidence in National Socialism. In 1932, and still in 1933, such

163

united action would have strengthened the courage to resist among the rank and file of professors. It might even have helped to create a broader front of resistance since the universities still enjoyed great intellectual prestige. But the critical moment passed without any action. Immediately upon Hitler's having been made chancellor on January 30, 1933, the Technische Hochschule Stuttgart hastened to pay homage by offering him an honorary doctor's degree which, however, he scorned to accept. On the other hand, the University of Bonn "found itself obliged," in 1936, to strike the name of Thomas Mann from its list of honorary doctors.[1] What followed then is well known: mass dismissals of racially and politically undesirable professors, and "political" appointments and promotions; academic self-government was lost; books were burned; manuscripts had to be submitted to political censorship; and compulsory courses on "national defense" and "racial science" were introduced.[2]

One may grant that a majority of German professors were at first troubled by these developments, yet the fact remains that they acquiesced in them. To protest individually, in the absence of united resistance, required more courage than the ordinary man possesses anywhere. Some had such courage. Theodor Litt, Karl Barth, Levin L. Schuecking, Julius Ebbinghaus and others spoke their minds in one way or another on the National-Socialist state while it was still in its infancy. Later when it had perfected itself in the art of suppression, the voices of protestants and dissenters were muffled beyond the smallest circle of trusted friends. Those who chose emigration, an act of pure virtue in fewer cases than has generally been supposed, cut themselves off from any effective influence within the country. A few of the others who stayed behind took their own lives, their hearts broken by the immortal shame or the inevitable catastrophe. But more typical was the lot of those who, sensitive but weak, could not decide the conflict between duty to their families and loyalty to their conscience. Pitiable and unheroic, they demonstrate the fate of scholar, scientist and educator in the modern dictatorial state which, once it is established, inexorably grinds down all human substance. It is necessary to understand their tragedy, if only to guard against self-righteousness on our part and against that lack of psychological realism out of which has been born the slogan of collective guilt. It is a phrase which obscures much and explains nothing. No military-government officer active in reorientation work in Germany today can expect to carry this difficult work forward if he bases it on the premise of collective guilt.

Yet these cases do not exhaust the variety of reasons for the acquiescence of German academic men. There were also the less scrupulous ones who successfully justified their silence and submission before their own conscience with the argument that they were employees of the state and owed allegiance to any constitutional government. Indeed, Nazi propaganda made capital of the fact that Hitler's accession to power had been in the form of a *legale Machtübernahme*, a shrewd slogan calculated precisely to allay whatever scruples might arise in the heart of the German bureaucrat. Professor Eugen Fischer, speaking in Berlin in November, 1933, attempted to persuade his colleagues and students that the manner in which the Nazi "revolution" had been accomplished justified complete trust in Hitler and his party. It was, he said, "a revolution in decency, a revolution in peace and order without hostages shot against a wall, without the flowing of blood, without barricades and civil war. There is no other nation in the world that could have done anything like it. A few weeks after the so-called revolution, our lecture halls were again full of students for the beginning of the regular summer term." [3]

Others again, not realizing that political neutrality had become indefensible, may simply have drifted into a situation whose gravity they failed to perceive. Devoid of political knowledge and acumen, they may have thought that it was only fair first to try and experiment with the new regime. For was one not bound in the name of science to await results before making any kind of summary judgment? Scientists whose work did not seem even remotely to touch upon political issues could persuade themselves that they would remain undisturbed. The totalitarian state might gag philosophy and history and corrupt literature and the arts. But if it desired military and technological efficiency, would it not have to leave science alone and even support it generously?

If these or similar ideas were in the minds of many German scientists, they only prove that the idea of truth as universal and indivisible had already been lost. It is unlikely that for any length of time science can flourish while in the humanities truth is politically prescribed. No one could have consented to such a separation if in his own mind the tradition of Kant or Humboldt remained alive and if he still acknowledged that *Wissenschaft* in its deeper sense is the search for the truth that shall make men free. But devoid of feelings of moral obligation, German scientists consented and contributed to the use of science in a war waged for the destruction of all but one nation. Nor had they enough forethought to consider that the victory of their own nation would be bought at the cost of extinguishing the freedom and responsibility of their own fellow citizens. In a dictator's world, even scientific inquiry, having rendered its destructive service, must eventually become suspect as the last source of critical thought and nonconformity.

In the latter part of 1933, the first year of Hitler's government, the universities like other fields of national life began to blossom with early converts and opportunists. Their propaganda and example helped to demoralize those who still straddled the fence. Ostentatious vows of allegiance to Hitler by a few nationally and internationally known professors gave the universities the appearance of readily "co-ordinating" themselves of their own free will. Such vows were made on the eve of the popular vote, November 12, 1933, by which Hitler asked the German people for a blanket approval of his policies, including the decisions to leave the League of Nations and the Disarmament Conference carried out a month earlier. Those who offered the vows accepted an invitation by the National Socialist Party to declare themselves publicly, "in perfect freedom" and "without the slightest pressure," in favor of Hitler and his "patriotic" action. The surgeon Sauerbruch, the philosopher Heidegger, and the historian of art Pinder, to name only the more widely known, obliged. Their endorsements of the new regime were at once printed and translated into five languages and dispatched to universities all over the Western world as evidence of the spontaneous agreement of German *Wissenschaft* with Hitler and his state.[4] The National Socialist Teachers' Union which published the vows was also able to obtain from nine hundred and sixty German scholars and scientists, most of them faculty members of universities and schools of university standing, signatures expressing agreement with those endorsements. It is not known how these signatures were obtained, what exactly the signees agreed to, and whether they actually saw the text of the statements. Disregarding these uncertainties, the nine hundred and sixty signatures indicate that roughly 11 per cent of the faculties of German universities and institutions of university standing had become Nazified by November, 1933. But figures here mean little. For statistics will not weigh or measure the capitulation of German science and scholarship.

Today, two years after the end of the war, nearly all German universities are again in operation. A few located in small towns escaped unscathed, the majority suffered heavy damage in libraries, laboratories and lecture halls. The teaching staffs of all of them have been drastically reduced by the denazification policy applied in their zones by the four occupying powers. Strenuous efforts are being made by academic senates to fill the numerous vacant chairs, for large numbers of students throng the universities. Among these students are temporizing, aimless veterans of many wars, and young uprooted and displaced people who still fight for the lost illusion of a middle-class life and career. Among them, also, are able and serious young men and women who after years of propaganda are starved for knowledge. Impatient with politics and political parties of any color, they study intently to become engineers and physicians and to devote themselves to the various tasks prescribed by the physical reconstruction of the country. Sober, factual and without illusions about the life ahead, this type of student is inclined to view the carnage and destruction through which he went as no other than natural catastrophes. This is a view which relieves him of the necessity of painful self-examination and of the difficulty of comprehending the meaning of recent history which he helped to make.

But it is precisely at these points that the educational work of the universities should begin. Staggering though the material problems are, those of human rehabilitation are greater. The visitor to Germany who talks to members of the academic faculties today does not, however, come away with the impression that they realize their enormous responsibility. He observes, too, that those teachers who are searching their own souls and who possess the tact, intelligence and courage to help the lost generation find its way back to a common humanity, are rare. It could be one of the most constructive policies of foreign military governments in Germany to help discover, encourage and promote to positions of intellectual leadership such teachers. On them depends to a very great extent the inner work of re-education.

Things as they now stand offer small reason for optimism or congratulation on our part. The universities operate, it is true; but they cannot be said to educate in the sense that this hour of history demands. Over-aged faculties and over-aged ministries control them. There is a tendency to resume traditions of teaching, thought and scholarship which long before the Nazis had become questionable. There is, too, a tendency toward academic life as usual. German universities still remain practically cut off from the outside intellectual world, and young men who are now entering an academic career under great difficulties say that they are suffocating in the stale air of stagnant traditions. Here and there a professor raises the question of a new society, a new education and a new type of man. But no new intellectual life has yet begun to stir, and no leadership has come to the front. The universities, crowded with students, offer a specious impression of activity. Educational and social planning, differing from zone to zone, is for the most part inadequate. The economic and financial future of Germany is dark. Her economists believe that the bottom of poverty has not yet been reached. Under such conditions it is difficult not to feel that the semblance of a regular academic life which the occupying powers themselves have been interested to create is a ghostly and unreal affair.

There is, however, no reason to despair. Only a short time has elapsed since the end of the war, and time is needed to reflect as well as to rebuild. The visitor, if he brings with him knowledge and understanding, finds no difficulty in meeting, among the many time-servers and confused petty men of yesterday, humble people who dare to hope for a united states of Europe with Germany as a member, who long for the community of civilized men and who are willing to expend what energies are left them from the daily struggle for existence on the re-education and rehabilitation of their own people. To show what is in their minds and how they look at the world today, I quote in conclusion some passages from one of the more significant rectoral addresses, delivered on September 25, 1945, at the reopening of the University of Marburg, by Professor Julius Ebbinghaus.

"A war which circled the globe ended only a short time ago. Germany, whose government loosed this war upon the world, has literally sacrificed her existence to the madness of her rulers and the blindness of her masses. What a bloodthirsty propaganda prophesied—that there would be no survivors among the defeated—is not *quite* true. And yet, beyond the millions of dead and the destruction of all our possessions, we have indeed forfeited our very existence. I mean our existence in the world of freedom, which is a community constituted in its own right and according to its own laws. Anxious patriots often asked each other, while the tyranny still lasted, what independent source of constructive power would remain in our people when every active and free expression had been stifled. That question has now been answered with terrible clarity. No such source remains, and Germany must accept her existence as a gift from the victors to enable her even to make peace."

"One fact remains unfortunately all too true. The German universities failed, while there was still time, to oppose publicly with all their power the destruction of *Wissenschaft* and of the democratic state. They failed to keep the beacon of freedom and right burning during the night of tyranny so that it could be seen by the entire world. However, one must remember that even then few scholars of international reputation remained whom the new tyrant would have hesitated to suppress. The many others, whose effectiveness lay only in their unity, lacked leaders. In many cases, too, they lacked political insight and manly resolution. The only possibility left them was to carry on a guerrilla warfare for the very survival of free inquiry in lecture halls and appointment committees, in the literature and in public addresses."

"If we are to hope that this will be an hour of promise, of a new beginning of science and philosophy in Germany, we must make certain to disperse the smoke screens in which they have been enveloped. The task facing the German people is, of course, one of reconstruction, and those who say that now we must look only ahead and not back, are certainly right. But let us not stop those who cart away the rubble of our ruins with the reproach that they are wasting their time in unproductive work when they should be hauling materials for new construction. The task of science and philosophy is to enlighten men, which is something eminently positive. Yet how can it be achieved unless the fallacies which obstruct the progress of knowledge have been cleared away? We stand before a youth in despair who accuse us of not having told them clearly and plainly why the political teaching, for which they now suffer, was false and perverse. Whether we so warned, or whether we must reproach ourselves for insufficient insight and courage to speak, are questions which each must answer before his own conscience. We shall have to reproach ourselves, however, if we fail *now* to speak plainly and tell those who are utterly confused and in despair why the gods they worshiped were false gods."

Professor Ebbinghaus, and with him the faculty of the University, then pledged themselves to kindle the spirit of free inquiry and criticism in the students so that all parroting of words would become intolerable to them; to teach them to think for themselves and to compare their judgments with those of others; to show them mankind in its greatness, but also in its smallness; to arouse distrust of human *hubris* and the pretenses of heroism; to help them understand that man can have no fatherland except one in which law and order prevail.

Professor Ebbinghaus ended with these words. "This is my pledge. It is not one which I have made thoughtlessly, or because the storm of democracy has swept over Germany. I do not know whether it is a democratic pledge, I only know that the intellectual discipline of many years has taught it to me. Whether or not my words have met your expectations, remember this, my young friends. For the present, neither affirm nor condemn. Clear your minds and open your hearts, and let us ask ourselves whether at the end of this unspeakable suffering there remains anything for men except to live together in accordance with the idea of mankind." [5]

NOTES

Chapter I, pp. 1–36

[1] The royal *Stiftungsbrief*, drawn up by Leibniz, also stated as aims of the institution the cultivation of the German language and church history. Cf. Adolf Harnack, *Geschichte der Akademie der Wissenschaften zu Berlin* (Berlin, 1910), vol. I, First Half, pp. 93–94.

[2] *Ibid.*, pp. 217 ff.

[3] For a brief history of the Collegium, cf. Max Lenz, *Geschichte der Königlichen Friedrich Wilhelms Universität zu Berlin* (Halle, 1910), vol. I, pp. 39 ff.

[4] On the intellectual life of Berlin at the end of the eighteenth century, cf. Wilhelm Dilthey, *Leben Schleiermachers* (Berlin, 1870), pp. 182–204.

[5] Reprinted in Rudolf Koepke, *Die Gründung der Universität Berlin* (Berlin, 1860).

[6] Specific references in Eduard Spranger, *Wilhelm von Humboldt und die Reform des Bildungswesens* (Berlin, 1910), Introduction. There is an extensive bibliography on the educational theory of that period in Kurt Grube, *Idee und Struktur einer rein-menschlichen Bildung* (Halle, 1934).

[7] The Minister's reprimanding letter and Kant's reply reprinted in Immanuel Kant, *Der Streit der Fakultäten* (Königsberg, 1798).

[8] *Lehrjahre*, Book V, chap. 3.

[9] This is the title of the English translation by Joseph Coulthart, London, 1854. The German title is *Ideen zu einem Versuch die Grenzen der Wirksamkeit des Staates zu bestimmen* (1792).

[10] *Ibid.* Quoted from Humboldt's *Gesammelte Schriften* (issued by the Preussische Akademie der Wissenschaften, 17 vols., Berlin, 1903–1936), vol. I, p. 117. All following quotations from Humboldt are from this edition unless otherwise stated. Translations are the author's.

[11] *Ibid.*, vol. I, p. 109.

[12] Quoted by Siegfried Kaehler, *Wilhelm von Humboldt und der Staat* (München, 1927), p. 512.

[13] *Gesammelte Schriften*, vol. X, p. 253.

[14] *Ibid.*, vol. I, pp. 74–75.

[15] Friedrich Meinecke, *Weltbürgertum und Nationalstaat* (München, 1908), chaps. 3 and 8.

[16] They are reprinted in Rudolf Koepke, *op. cit.*, pp. 154–159. For Wolf's outspoken criticism of the military aristocracy, referred to below, cf. Wilhelm Koerte, *Leben und Studien F. A. Wolfs* (Essen, 1833), vol. II, p. 4.

[17] Quotations in this paragraph from *Gesammelte Schriften*, vol. X, pp. 255, 253, 200.

[18] Georg Gottfried Gervinus, "Plan zur Reform der deutschen Universitäten 1835," in *Gesammelte kleine historische Schriften* (Karlsruhe, 1838).

[19] Cf. Schleiermacher's original recommendation in his *Gelegentliche Gedanken über Universitäten im deutschen Sinn*, 1808. Conveniently reprinted in

Eduard Spranger, *Über das Wesen der Universität* (Leipzig, 1919), p. 162. For a brief summary of the German policy of professorial appointments, cf. Friedrich Paulsen, *Die deutschen Universitäten und das Universitätsstudium* (Berlin, 1902), pp. 101–105.

[20] Cf. Max Lenz, *op. cit.*, vol. I, p. 79.

[21] Cf. Karl Viëtor, *Georg Büchner als Politiker* (Bern, 1939), pp. 12 ff. Forced to emigrate, Follen came to the United States and in 1825 became Instructor of German Literature and Language at Harvard University, but lost this position in 1835 because of his anti-slavery agitation. A street in Cambridge is named after him.

[22] Altenstein's letter recommending Hegel's appointment is reprinted in Lenz, *op. cit.*, vol. IV, pp. 334–335. On Ranke's appointment, *ibid.*, vol. II, First Half, pp. 255–258.

[23] Ranke, *Aufsätze zur eignen Lebensbeschreibung*, in *Sämmtliche Werke*, edited by Alfred Dove (Leipzig, 1890), vol. 53–54, p. 47.

[24] *Über die Verwandtschaft und den Unterschied der Historie und der Politik*, as reprinted by Erich Rothacker in *Leopold von Ranke: Das politische Gespräch und andere Schriftchen zur Wissenschaftslehre* (Halle, 1925), p. 50. Rothacker has collected in this little volume the most important writings of Ranke on the philosophy of history.

[25] *Sämmtliche Werke*, vol. 53–54, p. 174.

[26] Rothacker, *op. cit.*, p. 53.

[27] Quotations in this paragraph from Antoine Guilland, *Modern Germany and Her Historians* (New York, 1915), p. 86.

[28] *Sämmtliche Werke*, vol. 53–54, p. 219.

[29] Dedication to *Museum der Altertumswissenschaft*, edited by F. A. Wolf and Philipp Buttmann (1807), vol. I.

[30] Cf. Spranger's remarks in *Wilhelm von Humboldt und die Humanitätsidee* (Berlin, 1928), p. 467. Humboldt's ideas on the study of classical antiquity are to be found in letters to Wolf and in his essay, *Über das Studium des Altertums, und des Griechischen insbesondere*, in *Gesammelte Schriften*, vol. I.

[31] Friedrich Paulsen, in *German Education Past and Present* (New York, 1912), pp. 205–206, describes how dogmatic religious instruction was stressed and humanism denounced as irreligious even in the Prussian Gymnasia between 1840 and 1870.

[32] The very sharp attack on Treitschke's anti-Semitism is in *Auch ein Wort über unser Judentum* (1880), in *Reden und Aufsätze* (Berlin, 1905), pp. 410–426.

[33] Quoted by Lord Acton, *German Schools of History: Historical Essays and Studies* (London, 1908), p. 385.

[34] Quotations in this paragraph from G. P. Gooch, *History and Historians in the Nineteenth Century* (New York, 1935), pp. 140, 144.

[35] Cf. Jacob Grimm, *Über meine Entlassung* (Basel, 1838); and F. C. Dahlmann, *Zur Verständigung* (Basel, 1838).

[36] Quoted by Gooch, *op. cit.*, p. 150. For a brief summary of the diplomatic situation preceding the outbreak of the Franco-Prussian War, cf. A. J. Grant and H. Temperley, *Europe in the Nineteenth and Twentieth Centuries, 1789–1939* (New York, 1940).

[37] Quoted from Theobald Ziegler, *Die geistigen und sozialen Strömungen des 19. Jahrhunderts* (Berlin, 1911), p. 489.

Chapter II, pp. 37–56

[1] Quoted in Max Lenz, *Geschichte der Universität Berlin* (Berlin, 1910–1918), vol. II, p. 207.

[2] F. W. J. Schelling, *Über das Wesen deutscher Wissenschaft,* edited by Manfred Schroeter, vol. IV, p. 385 (Fragment aus dem Nachlass).

[3] Letter to Jacobi, Aug. 30, 1795, in *Briefwechsel J. G. Fichtes,* edited by Hans Schulz (1925), vol. I, p. 500.

[4] The German title is *Einige Vorlesungen über die Bestimmung des Gelehrten* (Jena, 1794). A second series of lectures of similar content he delivered at the University of Erlangen in 1815, under the title *Über das Wesen des Gelehrten und seine Erscheinungen im Gebiete der Freiheit.* They are reprinted together in the pocket series of Philipp Reclam, Leipzig.

[5] *Op. cit.*, p. 108.

[6] *Op. cit.*, p. 51.

[7] Thomas Carlyle, *Collected Works* (Chapman and Hall, 1869), vol. XII, p. 200.

[8] *Op. cit.*, p. 185.

[9] Cf. F. W. J. Schelling, *Vorlesungen über die Methode des akademischen Studiums* (1802); Henrik Steffens, *Über die Idee der Universitäten* (1809); Friedrich Schiller, *Über die ästhetische Erziehung des Menschen* (1795).

[10] *Deducirter Plan einer zu Berlin zu errichtenden höhern Lehranstalt,* as reprinted in Eduard Spranger, *Über das Wesen der Universität* (Leipzig, 1919), pp. 3–104.

[11] *Op. cit.*, § 7. Hereafter section number will be cited in the text following the quotation.

[12] Cf. p. 13.

[13] Second Address, § 14.

[14] J. G. Fichte, "Über die einzig mögliche Störung der akademischen Freiheit" (Rektoratsrede, Berlin, 1811), *Sämmtliche Werke,* vol. II.

[15] "Fichte und die nationale Idee," in Heinrich von Treitschke, *Ausgewählte Schriften* (Leipzig, 1907), vol. I.

[16] Friedrich Meinecke, *Weltbürgertum und Nationalstaat* (Berlin, 1908), p. 120.

[17] George Santayana, *Egotism in German Philosophy* (New York, 1940), chap. 7.

Chapter III, pp. 57–83

[1] Werner Siemens, *Das naturwissenschaftliche Zeitalter* (Rede, 1886).

[2] Schelling, *Werke.* Manfred Schroeter, ed. (München, 1927), vol. IV, pp. 182–183.

[3] Emil Du Bois-Reymond, *Reden* (Leipzig, 1912), vol. II, pp. 249 ff.

[4] F. Ueberweg, *Geschichte der Philosophie,* 12th ed. (Berlin, 1923), vol. IV, p. 40.

[5] Justus von Liebig, *Über das Studium der Naturwissenschaften und über den Zustand der Chemie in Preussen* (Braunschweig, 1844).

[6] Liebig, *ibid.*, p. 44.

[7] Hermann von Helmholtz, *Popular Lectures on Scientific Subjects*, 1st series, transl. by E. Atkinson (London, 1873), pp. 9–10. Of Hegel's ventures into science, his inaugural dissertation *De orbitis planetarum* (Jena, 1801), may here be mentioned, in which he denied, for philosophical reasons, the possible existence of a star in the gap between Mars and Jupiter. The following year a planetoid was discovered at the designated place. Cf. E. Zinner, *Geschichte der Sternkunde* (Berlin, 1931), p. 486. Hegel's abuse of Sir Isaac Newton in the *Enzyclopädie der philosophischen Wissenschaften* for his theory of colors is well known.

[8] Sir William Cecil Dampier, *A History of Science*, 3rd ed. (New York, 1942), p. 219.

[9] The faculty of philosophy in German universities developed out of the medieval Liberal Arts School as incorporated into the medieval university. The German "faculty" of philosophy may be compared to the American liberal arts college and the graduate school of arts and sciences combined.

[10] In 1873 the University of Munich and in 1875 the University of Würzburg subdivided their faculties of philosophy into two sections. Since both institutions, however, reserved to the entire faculty the right to vote on matters of general interest, the separation was not complete. In 1872 the University of Strassburg, reorganized after the Franco-Prussian War, established a separate mathematics-science department, but in this case the French tradition of separate higher schools seems to have been an influence.

[11] Quoted by A. W. Hofmann, *The Question of a Division of the Philosophical Faculty* (Boston, 1883), p. 12.

[12] Lothar Meyer, *Die Zukunft der deutschen Hochschulen und ihrer Vorbildungsanstalten* (Breslau, 1873).

[13] Notably on the initiative of Robert Ulich, now at Harvard University. See also his *Über Form und Gehalt der Technischen Hochschulen* (Berlin, 1932).

[14] Helmholtz, *On the Relation of Natural Science to Science in General.* E. Du Bois-Reymond, "Über Universitätseinrichtungen" (Rektoratsrede, Berlin, 1869), in *op. cit.* A. W. Hofmann (an important figure in the chemistry and the emerging industry of dyes), *op. cit.*

[15] Helmholtz, *ibid.*, p. 25.

[16] Helmholtz, *ibid.*, p. 32.

[17] "Fundamental concepts and comprehensive ideas he did not dispense," said Friedrich Paulsen in his *Autobiography* (New York, 1938), p. 214.

[18] Du Bois-Reymond, *op. cit.*, pp. 249 ff.

[19] Helmholtz, *op. cit.*, p. 29.

[20] Theodor Puschmann, *Die Bedeutung der Geschichte für die Medizin und die Naturwissenschaften* (1889—Tageblatt der 62. Versammlung deutscher Naturforscher und Ärzte, Heidelberg). Puschmann (1844–1899) wrote a *History of Medical Education*, transl. by Evan H. Hare, London, 1891.

[21] A wealth of observation on this matter may be found, for example, in Paulsen's *Autobiography*, chaps. 10, 11, 12. The abundance of bad and even atrociously bad teaching in a period that counted numerous great scholars and scientists—the above chapters cover the decade from 1866 to 1877—is astonishing.

22 "Germany is the only country in the world where the apothecary cannot make up a prescription without being conscious of the relation of his activity to the constitution of the universe." F. Lange, *Geschichte des Materialismus*, quoted by Dampier, *op. cit.*, p. 329.

23 Carl Vogt, *Köhlerglaube und Wissenschaft*, published in 1854, had its fourth edition in 1855. Ludwig Büchner's *Kraft und Stoff*, published in 1856, was the primer of the movement; nineteenth edition in 1898.

24 For Rudolf Virchow's views on science and education, cf. *Über den vermeintlichen Materialismus in den Naturwissenschaften* (1863); *Lernen und Forschen* (Rektoratsrede, Berlin, 1892); *Die Gründung der Berliner Universität und der Übergang aus dem philosophischen in das naturwissenschaftliche Zeitalter* (Universitätsrede, Berlin, 1892).

25 Dampier, *op. cit.*, p. 341.

26 Seventh edition in 1901 (15,000 copies); 400,000 copies by 1926 when the book had been translated into twenty-five languages.

27 Haeckel, *Riddle of the Universe*, English transl. by Joseph McCabe (New York, 1900), p. 381.

28 "Haeckel als Philosoph," in *Philosophia Militans* (Berlin, 1901).

29 *Monistische Sonntagspredigten*, Erste bis Vierte Reihe (Leipzig, 1911-1914).

Chapter IV, pp. 84-110

1 *Der werdende Nietzsche: Autobiographische Aufzeichnungen*, edited by Elizabeth Foerster Nietzsche (München, 1924), p. 427.

2 Cf. Ulrich von Wilamovitz Moellendorff, *Recollections*, transl. from the German by G. C. Richards (London, 1930), p. 150.

3 "David Strauss der Bekenner und der Schriftsteller," in *Nietzsches Gesammelte Werke* (Musarion Verlag, München, 1920-1929), vol. VI, p. 131. All quotations in this chapter are from this edition.

4 The best satire of the "culture Philistine" may be found in the opening pages of the work just cited. *Bildungsphilister* may not have been Nietzsche's invention. Rudolf Haym used it in his book *Die Romantische Schule* (1870), though for another sort of cultural pretender.

5 For this definition of education, cf. especially Nietzsche's notes to *Die Zukunft unsrer Bildungsanstalten*, vol. IV, pp. 127 ff. Relevant passages from other works are cited by George A. Morgan, Jr., *What Nietzsche Means* (Cambridge, Mass., 1943), pp. 217-219.

6 *Der alte und der neue Glaube* (Bonn, 1904), p. 84. This is a literal translation in which I have tried to perserve the miasma of the style and thought of the original.

7 It had six editions in 1872, seventeen editions by 1904.

8 Vol. VI, pp. 178-182.

9 Vol. XV, pp. 141-142. A similar "vivisection," too long to be quoted here, in *Schopenhauer als Erzieher*, vol. VII, pp. 100-105.

10 Chap. V will examine this particular influence of Nietzsche more fully.

11 Cf. Friedrich Paulsen, *German Education* (New York, 1912), pp. 203-205.

12 *Jenseits von Gut und Böse*, vol. XV, p. 143.

13 Burckhardt is best known for his book on *The Renaissance in Italy*. In 1943 James Hastings Nichols published the first English translation of Burck-

hardt's *Weltgeschichtliche Betrachtungen* under the title *Force and Freedom* (Pantheon Books, Inc.), with an excellent biographical introduction.

14 Nichols, *op. cit.*, p. 52.

15 Vol. VI, p. 181.

16 Cf. Karl Loewith, *Jacob Burckhardt* (Luzern, 1936), p. 363.

17 Burckhardt's *Werke, Gesammtausgabe,* edited by Felix Staehelin (Stuttgart, 1930), vol. VIII, p. 8.

18 First quotation in this paragraph from Nichols, *op. cit.*, p. 53; the others from Loewith, *op. cit.*, pp. 82–83.

19 Nichols, *op. cit.*, pp. 24, 40, 41, 43.

A similar prophecy by Nietzsche is quoted here from *Schopenhauer als Erzieher*, vol. VII, pp. 69-72. He sees, "in the growing rush and the disappearance of contemplation and simplicity from modern life, the symptoms of a complete uprooting of culture. The waters of religion retreat and leave behind pools and bogs. Nations once again divide in fierce hostility and burn to tear each other to pieces. The sciences, without measure and in blindly selfish devotion, dissolve and atomize old beliefs. The civilized classes and nations are swept away by the grand rush for contemptible wealth. Never was the world worldlier, never was it emptier of love and goodness. The learned and educated are no longer beacons or sanctuaries in this growing emptiness, but themselves grow daily more restive, thoughtless, and unloving. Everything, modern art and science included, prepares us for the coming barbarism. . . . Everything on earth will be decided by the crudest and most evil powers, by the selfishness of grasping men and military dictators. . . . But who will erect and preserve the image of man when men are so far gone that they feel like miserable worms or frightened dogs, because they have forgotten that image and sunk as low as beasts or even soulless mechanisms?"

20 Cf. Wilhelm Windelband, *Geschichte und Naturwissenschaft* (Strassburg, 1894); and Heinrich Rickert, *Kulturwissenschaft und Naturwissenschaft* (Freiburg, 1899).

21 Wilhelm Dilthey, *Gesammelte Schriften*, vol. VIII, p. 224. Generally significant in this connection is also the *Briefwechsel zwischen Dilthey und Yorck von Wartenburg, 1877–1897* (Halle, 1923).

22 For Dilthey's criticism of Nietzsche, cf. *ibid.*, vol. IV, p. 528.

23 *Philologie und Schulreform* (Prorektoratsrede, Göttingen, 1892).

24 Hermann Diels, *Das Elementum: Vorarbeit zu einem griechischen und lateinischen Thesaurus* (Leipzig, 1899).

25 Berlin, 1908. By Ludwig Hatvany, a Hungarian writer (1880–....).

26 For Schopenhauer's savage attack upon academic philosophy and his sarcasms about crabbed scholarship, cf. "Über die Universitätsphilosophie," *Sämmtliche Werke* (Brockhaus, Leipzig), vol. V (1938), and "Über Gelehrsamkeit und Gelehrte," *ibid.*, vol. VI (1939). For his denunciation of the journalistic corruption of German, cf. "Über Schriftstellerei und Stil," *ibid.*

Chapter V, pp. 111–130

1 All quotations from Langbehn are the author's translations from the 43rd edition (Verlag Hirschfeld, Leipzig, 1893), pp. 12, 76, 101, 69, 70, 71, 93.

2 Such are the judgments of *Der Grosse Brockhaus* and Meyer's *Konversa-*

tionslexikon. Also laudatory is Adolf Bartels, *Geschichte der deutschen Literatur* (1934); Biese, a widely used text, refrains from any criticism. Two notable exceptions to this torpor which I have run across are Theobald Ziegler, in *Die geistigen und sozialen Strömungen des 19. Jahrhunderts* (1911); and Eduard Engel, in *Deutsche Literaturgeschichte* (1913).

[3] Most revealing in this connection is the sophistry which Mr. Hauser employs when he wishes to prove that, in his youth, the Weimar of Goethe and Schiller "stank," that it "sucked the blood of vitality of the young," and that consequently, for the "large and significant German group," for which he claims to speak, "there is no road back to the old, the cultural, the harmless Germany" (p. 35). Compare this with the passage in which he speaks of the same sort of debunking of history in American schools ("George Washington had false teeth"). Only here it proves the rottenness of young America, while in the case of Mr. Hauser's young Germany it was a sign of health and vitality.

[4] *The Decline of the West,* trans. by Charles F. Atkinson (Alfred A. Knopf, Inc., New York, 1926), vol. I, p. 117.

[5] *Ibid.,* vol. II, p. 363.

[6] *Ibid.,* vol. II, p. 368.

[7] "Politische Pflichten der deutschen Jugend," in *Politische Schriften* (München, 1933), p. 147.

[8] "Pessimismus," in *Reden und Aufsätze* (München, 1937), p. 79.

[9] I find myself here in complete agreement with T. W. Adorno, in his essay on "Spengler Today," *Studies in Philosophy and Social Science* (New York, 1940), vol. IX, no. 2, pp. 305-325.

[10] "Nietzsche und sein Jahrhundert," in *Reden und Aufsätze.*

[11] Quoted from Helmut Frentzel, *George-Kreis und Geschichtswissenschaft,* p. 14. 1932.

[12] All quotations from *Dichter und Helden* (Heidelberg, 1923), pp. 44, 65.

[13] Cf. E. R. Bentley, *A Century of Hero Worship* (Philadelphia, 1944), pp. 223-228 and the Bibliography, for a discussion of the politics of the George circle.

[14] Cf. Graf Hermann von Keyserling, Introduction to *Creative Understanding* (New York, 1929), for a brief description of the Schule der Weisheit in Darmstadt.

[15] A lovely little pun by Gundolf is illustrative:

> Als Gottes Odem leiser ging,
> Schuf er den Grafen Geyserling.

[16] Sören Kierkegaard, *Gesammelte Werke* (Jena, 1910), vol. VII, p. 29.

[17] Cf. Karl Loewith, *Kierkegaard und Nietzsche* (Frankfurt, 1933), for a good brief comparison of these two philosophers.

[18] Wahl, *Etudes Kierkegaardiennes* (Paris, 1938), p. 468.

[19] *The War Against the West* (New York, 1938), p. 282.

[20] For Heidegger's political conversion, see the rectoral address *Die Selbstbehauptung der deutschen Universität* (Freiburg, 1933). Also his "Vow of Allegiance" in *Bekenntnis der Professoren an den deutschen Universitäten und Hochschulen zu Adolf Hitler und dem nationalsozialistischen Staat* (Dresden, 1933).

[21] *Works* (Centenary edition, Oxford, 1928-1937), vol. XXI, p. 186.

[22] Erich Kahler wrote this pamphlet in reply to Max Weber's address on *Wissenschaft als Beruf* (1919), which is discussed in the following chapter. This controversy drew further comments from Artur Salz, *Für die Wissen-*

schaft gegen die Gebildeten unter ihren Verächtern (1921); Max Scheler, *Schriften zur Soziologie und Weltanschauungslehre* (Leipzig, 1932), vol. I, pp. 1–25; Ernst Troeltsch, "Die Revolution in der Wissenschaft," *Gesammelte Schriften* (Tübingen, 1925), vol. IV, pp. 653–677.

Chapter VI, pp. 131–162

[1] The speech was entitled "Wissenschaft als Beruf"; published in Weber, *Gesammelte Aufsätze zur Wissenschaftslehre* (Tübingen, 1922).

[2] Quoted by Karl Loewith in "Max Weber und Karl Marx," *Archiv für Sozialwissenschaft und Sozialpolitik*, vol. LXVII, no. 1, p. 93 (March, 1932).

[3] "Wissenschaft als Beruf," p. 554.

[4] Here is the most striking contrast between Weber and certain followers of the educational philosophy of John Dewey in this country.

[5] For example "Die Objektivität sozialwissenschaftlicher und sozialpolitischer Erkenntnis" and "Der Sinn der 'Wertfreiheit' der soziologischen und ökonomischen Wissenschaften," in *Gesammelte Aufsätze zur Wissenschaftslehre*.

[6] The best study of the problems of the overcrowding of higher education and of unemployment among its graduates is that of Walter M. Kotschnig, *Unemployment in the Learned Professions* (London, 1937). A brief but excellent account is given by Martin Doerne, "Problems of the German University," in *The University in a Changing World*, ed. by W. M. Kotschnig and E. Prys (London, 1932).

[7] Kotschnig, *op. cit.*, p. 57.

[8] See especially Doerne, *op. cit.*

[9] Cf. especially the end of his essay on "Der Bourgeois und die religiösen Mächte," in *Abhandlungen und Aufsätze* (Leipzig, 1915), vol. II.

[10] *Die Wissensformen und die Gesellschaft* (Leipzig, 1926), p. 498.

[11] "Der Philosophische Pragmatismus," in *Die Wissensformen und die Gesellschaft*, pp. 259–299.

[12] "Probleme einer Soziologie des Wissens," in *Die Wissensformen und die Gesellschaft*, p. 228. It may be noted that Scheler was convinced in the 1920's that the technical leadership of Europe, its increase of population, and its decisive political role in world relations were matters of the past. But his conclusions were not pessimistic. Scattered passages in his writings give the impression that he thought Europe would now have the time to develop her intellectual and spiritual resources. That could be her important role in world culture at the time when other continents would be increasingly absorbed in technology and industry.

[13] Cf. *Schriften zur Soziologie und Weltanschauungslehre* (Leipzig, 1923), vol. I.

[14] *Die Stellung des Menschen im Kosmos* (Darmstadt, 1928), p. 112.

[15] "Probleme einer Soziologie des Wissens," p. 90.

[16] Cf. Walter Krivitsky, *In Stalin's Secret Service* (New York, 1939).

[17] Scheler was here indebted to certain ideas of Paul Natorp, who had begun to direct, at the University of Marburg, an adult education center of the sort here described. The *Lessinghochschule* in Berlin, founded in 1915, developed into a modern peoples' university after the end of World War I in the spirit of Scheler's ideal.

[18] *German Philosophy and Politics* (G. P. Putnam's Sons, New York, 1942).
[19] *Ibid.*, p. 90.
[20] *Ibid.*, p. 19.
[21] *Ibid.*, p. 30.
[22] "Challenge to Liberal Thought," *Fortune*, August, 1944, p. 188.
[23] To explain how this became a German trait, it would be necessary to go back in German history as far as the Reformation and the Thirty Years' War, the social consequences of which had much to do with destroying the wealth, political independence, and religious integrity of the German middle class and citizenry. It would have been more in harmony with Dewey's own beliefs, had he sought there the origin of certain unfortunate German traits rather than in Kant who has hardly been a "popular" philosopher.

Epilogue, pp. 163–171

[1] Mann's moving reply, a cultural document of the first order, is reprinted in Thomas Mann, *Achtung Europa! Aufsätze zur Zeit* (New York, 1938), pp. 97–109.
[2] The effects of National Socialism on the German universities during the first four years are discussed by E. Y. Hartshorne, *The German Universities and National Socialism* (Cambridge, Mass., 1937).
[3] *Bekenntnis der Professoren an den deutschen Universitäten und Hochschulen zu Adolf Hitler und dem nationalsozialistischen Staat* (Dresden, 1933).
[4] *Ibid.*
[5] For the translation of the larger part of Professor Ebbinghaus's address, cf. my article, "A German University Reopens," *Harvard Educational Review*, Spring, 1946. The German text of the address is reprinted in: Julius Ebbinghaus, *Zu Deutschlands Schicksalswende*. Frankfurt am Main. 1946.

INDEX

A

Académie des Sciences et Belles-
Lettres (Berlin), 6
Acton, Lord, 26
Altenstein, Karl, 24, 25
Aristotle, 30, 74
Arndt, Ernst Moritz, 22

B

Baeumler, Alfred, 111
Barth, Karl, 164
Basle, University of, 84, 85, 97, 100,
101, 104
Becker, Carl Heinrich, 147
Beloch, Julius, 102
Bergson, Henri, 124–125
Berlin, University of, Chap. I, II,
passim; also 59, 101, 109, 146
Bernhardi, Friedrich von, 159
Bertram, Ernst, 121, 122–123
Beyme, Karl Friedrich, 5, 42
Bismarck, Prince, 32, 33, 34, 35, 36, 87,
119
Böckh, August, 28, 31
Bonn, University of, 22, 23, 57, 85,
164
Brentano, Lujo, 35
Breslau, University of, 32
Büchner, Ludwig, 78
Bunsen, Robert, 64
Burckhardt, Jacob, 28, 34, 84, 95,
100–104, 106
Burke, Edmund, 26
Burschenschaften, 21, 22

C

Carlyle, Thomas, 41–42, 84, 114
Chamberlain, Houston Stewart, 114
Collège de France, 151
Collegium Medico-Chirurgicum, Ber-
lin, 4
Comte, Auguste, 153

D

Dahlmann, F. C., 34
Dampier, Sir William Cecil, 63
Darwin, Charles, 80
Dehn, Fritz, 163
Deutscher Hochschulverband, 163
Dewey, John, 158–161
Diels, Hermann, 95, 106, 108–109
Dilthey, Wilhelm, 34, 95, 100, 105–106
Dresden, *Technische Hochschule,* 69
Droysen, J. G., 25, 32, 33
Du Bois-Reymond, Emil, 66, 69, 73,
79–80
Du Bois-Reymond, Paul, 66

E

Ebbinghaus, Julius, 164, 169–171
Emerson, R. W., 42
Engel, J. J., 5, 18
Erlangen, University of, 60

F

Fichte, J. G., Chap. II *passim;* also
18, 24, 29, 89, 133, 142, 159
Fischer, Eugen, 165
Fischer, Kuno, 32
Follen, Karl, 21
Frankfurt (Main), University of, 121
Frankfurt (Oder), University of, 3
Frederick II (The Great), King of
Prussia, 6, 7, 17, 21
Frederick William I, King of Prussia,
3, 4
Frederick William III, King of Prussia,
20, 24
Frederick William IV, King of Prussia,
24, 31, 59
Freiburg, University of, 128

G

Gay-Lussac, J. L., 60
George, Stefan, 85, 112, 119–120